Planet Cake

Acknowledgments

The first people I need to thank are our students who, since the inception of our decorating workshops have inspired me to write this book. They have helped me to maintain my passion for decorating by watching theirs bloom — a truly wonderful gift. My second thank you is to Murdoch Books and my editor Kristin Buesing for giving me the wonderful opportunity to bring this book to life and for gracing *Planet Cake* with the talents of photographer Natasha Milne and food stylist Kate Brown, who together helped translate our cakes into the delectable images you see before you.

The cakes and content in this book would never have come to fruition without the hard work, talent, and support of my incredibly dedicated and professional staff, past and present, who have brainstormed with me, torn their hair out with me, offered their talents, and laughed with me. There are two staff in particular who deserve a special thank you.

Firstly I would like to thank Anna Maria Roche who has worked with me on this book. Not only has she been happy to manage all the "boring" aspects of creating a book, but as a talented decorator she has donated all the cupcake designs that are featured in this book. Anna Maria, thank you so much for your contributions and for your enthusiasm, which can never be extinguished no matter how tedious things become.

The second important contributor to this book is Margaret Carter. Her stunning illustrations grace every cake, and her talent and imagination are the very foundations of Planet Cake. Margie, few words can express how much joy I gain from our creative partnership: thank you so much for your talent and contribution.

Other important members of our team I would like to thank are Handi Mulyana for his amazing teaching ability and his help in creating our course curriculum. I want to thank our resident pastry chef extraordinaire, Jessica Pedemont, for trialling and developing all the recipes. Also Ritsuko Sato, for her design contributions and the wonderful Japanese flavor the cakes have. I need to pay special homage to our good friend and fellow decorator Greg Cleary for the best fondant recipe in the universe and for all his support and help.

Finally, I would like to thank my business partner, husband, and tireless supporter, Billy Cutler. Without his extraordinary support, not only would this book not have been possible, but Planet Cake would not be what it is today. For all the thank yous I never uttered, I will make this the official one: thank you.

Planet Cake

Planet Cake

A beginner's guide to decorating incredible cakes

Paris Cutler

METRO BOOKS
New York

Contents

Welcome to Planet Cake

Long before Planet Cake was born, a decorated cake gave me my first real career break. Straight from school and only 18 years old, I was working as a runner in one of Sydney's top stockbroking firms. I ran all over town delivering trading dockets, constantly exhausted and earning a very low wage but seeing it as an opportunity for greater things. After six months that opportunity came when I was invited, along with everyone at the firm, to a 60th birthday party for one of the senior partners. The rumor was that if you could impress a partner, your career would be fast-tracked straight to the trading floor. My delight quickly turned to unease when everyone began discussing their gifts (I can remember through my haze of anxiety that a gold Rolex was mentioned). I could barely afford my rent let alone an extravagant present.

However, I discovered that the senior partner loved Harley Davidson motorbikes, so I decided to make him a very special cake. This cake was crudely designed and poorly executed and I felt sick with embarrassment when I arrived at the party, only to be overwhelmed by his response. My motorbike cake was placed as the party centrepiece, I became the belle of the ball, and from that moment the senior partner took an active interest in my career. It was an amazing lesson in what giving a little time and imagination can achieve in a material world where people can buy anything they want. However, much to the dismay of my family, I left my big break in stockbroking (I found myself reading craft magazines instead of financial reports and spent my lunch hours talking to the florist about her displays for the company foyer rather than networking with clients) and fell, quite by accident, into my dream job.

When I first stumbled across Planet Cake in 2003 it was a tiny little shop located down a Sydney side street and had already been operating virtually unchanged for seven years. The shop was originally established by Margie Carter, a world-class cake decorator who we are fortunate enough to still have at Planet Cake as Artistic Director. The original store was painted electric blue and had a dusty figurine of Astro Boy in the front window and cupids on the walls; in terms of size it was not much bigger than my daughter's bedroom. However, inside was a magical world of cakes. It was this atmosphere of creativity and the exceptional quality of the work that persuaded me to invest in the business and become owner of Planet Cake.

From these modest beginnings we've moved to a much larger production kitchen (in which we've created many "celebrity" wedding cakes, including that of Nicole Kidman and Keith Urban). Our kitchen also serves as a classroom: we began holding decorating workshops in 2004 and have now taught hundreds of students, and trained and employed many talented cake decorators. We are a true team, with a specialist in every area: novelty, figurines, sugar flowers, decorating, and wedding cakes. It is the creativity and high-quality techniques of this team that we want to share with you in this book.

The best starting point

Unbelievably, Planet Cake exports from Sydney as far afield as Europe and South America. This is entirely due to the way we set up our cakes and our rolled (or ready-to-use) fondant icing, which does not require refrigeration. I constantly receive questions from aspiring decorators wanting to know how we achieve the sharp edges on our cakes, and keep them moist and delicious. If you have ever eaten a dry novelty cake with unpalatable thick icing, then you'll appreciate the method I'm going to show you to avoid that.

Spending the extra time to make sure your cake is perfectly sculpted and covered with a completely smooth layer of chocolate ganache before you ice it allows you to use one layer of thin icing. It is this that will give you the sharp edges and crisp look every cake decorator craves. This book is set out in a specific order so that you spend time learning to ganache and cover a cake perfectly before moving on to the top layer of decorating. This is the same method we use to train students in our kitchen classroom.

Our philosophy is that if you cannot set up your cake properly and cover it expertly then, no matter how brilliant and creative your decorating, the cake will always look clunky and unprofessional, and it will probably taste dry as well. There really is no secret to becoming a great cake decorator other than solid skills in ganaching and covering, an eye for color and proportion, practice, and patience. In a commercial environment, trainee cake decorators are taught by shape and that is the method we will follow in this book. As a new trainee at Planet Cake you would spend a year focusing on ganaching and covering cakes, mastering increasingly difficult shapes as you advance, and that is how we have set out our chapters. The program is designed so that you will gain different skills and re-enforce techniques already learnt as the cakes become progressively more advanced.

Cupcakes and round cakes are where beginners should start. In these chapters you will learn the crucial decorating skills that will form the basis of the rest of your learning. Leaping in and decorating a square cake with no prior experience can be a frustrating exercise. The square has a few tricks regarding angles that are much better mastered once you have experience in covering round cakes with rolled fondant icing.

It's very tempting to want to rush into making a groovy-shaped or novelty cake but your results will be much higher (and your stress levels much lower) if you have had prior experience with round and square cakes. So, if you start with cupcakes or round cakes and methodically work through each chapter, you will actually be completing the same training as a trainee at Planet Cake.

Have fun, and enjoy the results.

How to use this book

The first two chapters of this book will provide you with several delicious cake and icing recipes. These are the same cakes that we use at Planet Cake, so we know the recipes work well, the cakes are firm enough to give a good basis for decorating, and they store well. The glossary and equipment pages will give you photographic reference for stocking your kitchen. The techniques chapter will then lead you through the basics of cake decorating, giving you hints and tips and also a section on troubleshooting when something goes wrong.

Ganache

Have a good look at how we set-up our cakes with ganache to achieve very clean and sharp edges. Ganache also tastes much better than the buttercream that some people use, and the cake keeps for much longer.

Rolled fondant icing

At Planet Cake we only use rolled fondant icing (also known as ready-to-use icing), which finishes with a nice satin shine and is very reliable. We always buy this ready made, but if you did want to make your own see the recipe on page 33. Because we set up the cakes first with a smooth hard layer of ganache that hides any imperfections and gives a perfect foundation, this allows us to use only a thin layer of fondant icing.

Using a pasta machine

One of our "tricks" at Planet Cake is to use a pasta machine for rolling out icing evenly. If you don't already own a pasta machine, buy a cheap one and you'll find it much easier than the traditional rolling pin. You can even use the spaghetti-making setting to make tassels for the flag cake (page 139).

Using a flexi-scraper

Another useful item you will discover is our flexi-scraper (one of our proudest inventions!). You can make this out of firm plastic, so that it is firm but remains flexible (see glossary, page 17). We use the flexi-scraper for buffing and polishing the icing, which is the "secret" to the sharp edges that give our cakes their professional look.

Storing and transporting your cake

Keep your decorated cake away from water as this will "burn" the icing and leave it stained. Sunlight will fade the color of the icing and heat will soften it, so any decorations may melt or droop. However, never put the iced cake in the fridge as the damp environment will make the icing sweat. Store the finished cake in a cake box, putting a nonslip rubber mat under the cake board to prevent the cake moving. To prevent cupcakes from moving, stick them on the cake board with royal icing.

Essential planning and preparation

Planning

Two weeks prior to making your cake, check through the recipe to ensure you have all the materials and ingredients required.

Making and decorating cakes always takes longer than you think, and for an enjoyable experience it is important to be as organized as possible. If you are making a cake for a special event, make sure you have all the materials and equipment necessary. Some specialist products or equipment might not always be in stock and may require ordering in advance from a supplier.

Designing

The designs in this book can be followed to the letter or, as you gain more confidence, tailored to your own needs. Once you have learnt the techniques, they are easily adapted. Obviously, the easiest thing to change is the color palette. However, you can also change the cut-outs or decoration detail; for example the Exploding star cake (page 122) can be easily changed to hearts for Valentine's Day or an engagement party, and the Flag cake (page 139) also works well as the flag of a country or sports team.

Note: Some designs use nonedible elements, such as toothpicks or plastic tubing, that need removing before the cake is served.

Preparing the work space

I cannot emphasize enough how important it is to prepare your work space before you start. Make sure you have everything you require, including: room in the freezer if you're going to freeze your cake before decorating; adequate bench space and boards; all the equipment and ingredients to hand such as cornstarch for lightly dusting the work surface and plastic sheets. Rolled fondant icing dries out very quickly and, therefore, always wrap the icing in plastic or, if already rolled, cover it with a plastic sheet.

The three-day rule

The three-day rule is very important. If you want to create a wonderful, professional-looking cake, this is the time that it requires and it is futile (and stressful) to try to hurry it. Cakes that are not given time to cool, or ganache that has not been allowed to set properly, will make poor foundations for the rest of the decoration.

Day 1: Bake your basic cake and allow adequate time for it to cool. Most of our basic cakes (pages 22–27) can be kept for up to a week in an airtight container, or in the freezer for 2 months before decorating.

Day 2: Cut and ganache the cake (page 36) and allow adequate time for the ganache to set.

Day 3: Decorate the cake.

This is the basic set of equipment you will need to make and decorate cakes. You don't need to buy all these tools at once — you might prefer to start with some simple items, such as a couple of icing tips for decorating, which can also be used as circle cutters, and a rolling pin, and then slowly build up your tool box.

Icing equipment

1. Flour shaker
2. Pizza wheel
3. Small knife
4. Large rolling pin
5. Icing smoothers in different sizes
6. Scissors
7. Zip-lock bags
8. Flexi-scraper
9. Turntable (for TV)

Edible decorations and materials

1. Rolled fondant icing
2. Decorating alcohol
3. Tylose powder
4. Coloring paste
5. Florist tape
6. Piping gel
7. Coloring paste
8. Dragees
9. Edible glitter
10. Edible gold dust
11. Instant royal icing
12. Liquid coloring
13. Container for liquids
14. Cornstarch

Ganaching tools

1. Plastic jug
2. Cleaning cloth
3. Palette knives
4. Large palette knife
5. Serrated or bread knife
6. Masonite set-up and display cake boards
7. Pastry brush
8. Turntable (for TV)
9. Nonslip rubber mat
10. Waxed paper
11. DIY board
12. Pencils (2B)
13. Scraper

Decorating equipment

1. Wire
2. Alphabet cutters
3. Small rolling pin
4.+10. Broad and
    fine paintbrushes
5. Serrated dough wheel
6. Stitching tool
7. Balling tool
8. Frilling tool
9. Cotton wool
11. Tape measure
12. Plastic paint palette
13. Toothpicks
14. Ruler
15. Small rolling pin
16. Waxed paper
17. Wooden skewers
18. Dowel
19. Icing tips and coupler
20. Icing bag
21. Flower cutter
22. Dropper
23. Star cutters
24. Aquarium tubing
25. Nonslip rubber mat
26. Pasta machine
27. Circle cutters

Glossary

Many items listed here are available from specialist cake-decorating suppliers. Some of the more everyday bits can be bought at the supermarket or cookware shops.

Acetate film is often described as plastic film or sheeting. This general-purpose plastic is an industry standard in graphic arts, packaging, printing and for overlays.

Aquarium tubing can be found in hardware stores or aquarium shops. This plastic tubing is inexpensive, comes in different diameters and has many different uses.

Balling tool This long plastic stick has a ball at either end. Use it to make round indentations and smooth curves in modelling or to shape flower petals.

Cachous or **dragees** are round, edible sugar balls coated with silver or gold which are used for decorative purposes.

Cake boards are usually made from silver or gold masonite and are available from cake-decorating supply shops.

Set-up cake boards are the same size as the cake (for example, 9-inch round cake on a 9-inch round board) and they operate as a guide for ganaching and a way to easily handle the cake and not stain the display board.

The display cake board or "final" board is the larger board the cake is placed on as part of its display; the display board is 4 to 6 inches larger than the cake.

Cake dowels are long, thin, solid, cylindrical plastic or wooden pillars, pointed at one end.

They are pushed into cakes to support pillars for holding tiered cakes. They are also useful for moulding and modelling. If they are to be inserted into the cake we recommend covering the dowel with food-safe tape.

Cornstarch is used in cake decorating for dusting the work surface when rolling out icing. It must be used sparingly, as it can dry the icing out, but it is finer to use than icing sugar.

Couverture is a natural, sweet chocolate containing no added fats other than natural cocoa butter. It is used for dipping, molding, coating, and similar purposes. Use semisweet chocolate as subtitute if unavailable.

Cutters are available in different sizes and shapes and often come in sets, in plastic or stainless steel.

Decorating alcohol has 5 per cent rose essence and is used for painting and removing icing stains. Vodka can be used as a substitute.

DIY cake board is a waxed cardboard template used as a substitute set-up board when decorating an unusual shape. For example, the Paint tube cake (page 172) requires you to make your own wax DIY board from the templates provided (see pages 186-89).

Edible glitter is available in an array of colors and is usually applied with water or piping gel.

Edible glue is also known as sugar glue. It is used to glue together dry pieces of icing such as securing dried modeling icing figurines to a dried cake. If both or one of the pieces were still soft, they could be stuck with just water or egg white, so often edible glue is not necessary.

Flexi-scraper is a Planet Cake invention. We use either unused X-ray film, which can be hard to get, or a thin plastic such as acetate, computer film or the plastic used for bendy display folders (the ones with the plastic sleeves inside). Cut the plastic to a rectangle a little larger than the palm of your hand, round the edges using scissors, and disinfect the plastic.

Florist tape can be twisted on its own to create an effect, but it can also be used to cover wires or dowels before inserting into the cake. Some are coated with a green paper.

Food color Paste coloring is the most concentrated of food colors. Mix this paste directly into your fondant icing to color it, or mix it with alcohol to paint with. Liquid coloring is similar but less intense.

Frilling tool This tool is part of a set called "modeling tools". It is used to frill soft surfaces such as sugar paste, modelling paste, flower paste, or marzipan.

Ganache is a mixture of chocolate and cream. It can be made with semisweet, milk, or white chocolate, and is used as a filling or icing for cakes.

Glaze is a product or mixture that gives a shiny appearance to cakes or decorations.

Glycerine is a colorless, odorless, syrupy liquid made from fats and oils and used to retain moisture and add sweetness to foods. Stir into icing to restore consistency or use to soften fondant or royal icing. It can also be used to soften dried icing colors.

Marzipan or almond paste is made from ground blanched almonds and confectioners' sugar. It is used as a very thin layer on fruit cakes before they are covered with royal icing or sugar paste. Marzipan can also be used for making flowers and fruit.

Nonslip rubber mats are perfect for placing under your turntable or cake to prevent slipping. A mat is also great underneath the cake when placing it in a cake box for transport.

Paintbrushes Fine paintbrushes can be used for painting, brushing crumbs, or confectioners' sugar out of tricky corners, as well as applying powdered or liquid colors. Broad brushes are useful for cleaning debris off the cake board.

Palette knife The cranked palette knife is usually a plastic-handled knife with a bend (crank) in it, and is used to ganache cakes and cupcakes. The palette knife is a flat, metal palette knife used to smooth ganache, and can also be handy to transfer the cake from a temp board to the display board. Both types come in large and small sizes.

Parchment bag is a disposable decorating bag formed from a parchment paper triangle.

Pasta machine is also called a pasta maker. It is used for making homemade pasta and is useful to roll out icing as it provides a consistent thickness and rolls the icing perfectly.

Piping gel is a clear sticky gel that becomes fluid when warmed. It can be colored for icing on dry sugar paste or royal icing. It maintains a shiny, wet look when set. Also known as piping jelly.

Powders and dusts are available in petal, pearl, sparkle and lustre finishes. Some decorators mix the powder with decorating alcohol and apply the color directly. The lustre and pearl powders create a luminous effect to sugar flowers.

Rolled fondant icing Also called ready-to-use, plastic icing, sugar paste, and fondant, it is a dough-like icing that is rolled out, draped over the cake and then smoothed down. This icing is used to cover cakes and cupcakes.

The basic ingredient of fondant is confectioners' sugar with the addition of gelatin, corn syrup (glucose) and glycerine to provide a malleable sweet paste. Fondant gives the cake a beautiful, porcelain-like surface that can be painted, piped, quilted, cut out, or stamped. Fondant usually comes in white or ivory and can be tinted to any color of the rainbow. It is also used to model and cut three–dimensional shapes for decoration, such as ribbons, bows, and cut-outs. Good-quality fondant is costly but worth buying.

Rolling pins A small rolling pin is ideal for small projects and rolling out small pieces of icing. You can buy a fancy one from a cake-decorating supplier, but the most prized small rolling pins at Planet Cake are those found in children's baking sets!

A large rolling pin is a long, smooth cylindrical roller mainly used to roll out pastry. A variety of types are available: without handles, with integral handles, or Planet Cake's favorite, with handles that are attached to a central rod in the roller. Rolling pins are usually made from wood but can also be made from marble or silicon. Choose a rolling pin you are comfortable with.

Royal icing is a mixture of egg white or albumen and confectioners' sugar. It can be spread over cakes and boards and sets very hard. It is also used for icing bags. You can buy instant royal icing mixes where you just have to add water, or you can make your own using the recipe on page 33.

Scraper Best made of stainless steel, a side scraper is a flat piece of metal or plastic with a straight side that is used for scraping the excess ganache off the side of a cake when you are preparing and filling it. Metal scrapers can be sourced from cake-decorating suppliers and the internet. If you don't have a scraper you can use a metal ruler. Plastic scrapers are also fine to use.

Smoothers are also called "paddles." These rectangular, flat plastic paddles with handles are used for pressing the air bubbles out of fondant icing and rubbing it to a smooth shiny finish. For covering cakes you always need at least two smoothers.

Stitching tool, more properly known as a tracing wheel, is an instrument with serrated teeth on a wheel attached to a handle. A stitching tool is used in sewing to transfer markings from patterns onto fabric, but this tool also makes a perfect stitching effect in rolled fondant icing. There are two basic types of tracing wheels available, one with a serrated edge and one with a smooth edge. You need to buy the serrated edged tracing wheel, which is available from haberdashers.

Syrup, sugar syrup or soaking syrup is a mixture made from equal amounts of boiled water and jam (recipe page 32). The syrup is brushed over the cut surfaces of cakes to prevent them drying out before icing. Syrup can be flavored with alcohol such as Cointreau (orange liqueur).

Tips and coupler for decorations Sometimes called decorating tubes or tips, the tips are specially shaped with open-ends. The size and shape of the opening determines the type of decorations the tip will produce. The coupler sits between the icing bag and tip. You can screw the tip onto the coupler and easily change between different sizes and shapes without changing the icing bag.

Turntable is a useful tool for when you are coating cakes with royal icing or rolled icing as it allows you to approach the cake from all sides. You can just buy a turntable from a cake-decorating store but at Planet Cake we actually like to use the type that you would put under a TV set.

Tylose powder can be mixed into rolled fondant, marzipan, or royal icing, and forms a strong modelling paste that dries hard. Tylose powder can also be mixed with a small amount of water to make thick and strong edible glue.

Wire is available from cake-decorating stores. It comes in different thicknesses called gauges, and sometimes it is covered with paper. Use no. 22 gauge for the Exploding star cake (page 122).

Cake recipes

The wonderful thing about these cakes is that they actually taste great. Your cakes are going to taste as magnificent as they look.

Vanilla cupcakes

Makes 12 cupcakes

¾ cup unsalted butter, softened
¾ cup superfine sugar
1 teaspoon natural vanilla extract
1 teaspoon grated lemon zest
1 tablespoon Madeira (optional)
2 eggs
1 cup self-rising flour
⅔ cup all-purpose flour
¾ cup plus 2 tablespoons milk

1. Preheat the oven to 350°F. Line a 12-cup cupcake tin with paper liners.

2. Beat the butter, sugar, vanilla, lemon zest, and a pinch of salt with electric beaters until pale and fluffy. Add the Madeira and beat until well combined. Add the eggs one at a time, beating well after each addition.

3. Sift the flours together. Using a wooden spoon, fold the flour and milk alternately into the creamed mixture.

4. Spoon into the paper liners and bake for 20 to 25 minutes, or until a skewer comes out clean when poked into the center of a cake.

5. Leave the cupcakes in the tin for 5 minutes, then remove them and allow the cakes to cool on a wire rack.

Storage: Keep the cupcakes in an airtight container in the fridge for up to two days, or freeze for up to 1 month.

Chocolate mud cake

Makes one 9-inch round cake or
one 8-inch square cake

¾ cup plus 2½ tablespoons butter
7¾ oz semisweet chocolate,
chopped
½ cup instant coffee
½ cup plus ⅓ cup self-rising flour
½ cup plus ⅓ cup all-purpose flour
⅓ cup unsweetened cocoa powder
½ teaspoon baking soda
1¾ cups superfine sugar
4 eggs, lightly beaten
7 teaspoons vegetable oil
7 tablespoons buttermilk

1. Preheat the oven to 325°F. Grease the cake pan and line the bottom and sides with a collar of waxed paper that extends ¾ inch above the top of the pan.

2. Put the butter, chocolate and coffee in a saucepan with ⅔ cup of water and stir over low heat until melted, then remove from the heat.

3. Sift the flours, cocoa, and baking soda into a large bowl. Stir in the sugar and make a well in the center. Add the combined egg, oil, and buttermilk and the chocolate mixture, stirring with a large spoon until completely combined.

4. Pour the mixture into the pan and bake for 1 hour 40 minutes, or until a skewer poked into the center of the cake comes out clean, though it may be a little sticky. Leave the cake in the pan until cold.

Storage: Keep the cake in an airtight container in the fridge for up to 3 weeks, or freeze for up to 2 months.

Carrot cake

Makes one 9-inch round cake or one 8-inch square cake

1 cup self-rising flour
1 cup all-purpose flour
2 teaspoons ground cinnamon
1 teaspoon ground ginger
½ teaspoon ground nutmeg
1 teaspoon baking soda
¾ cup plus 2 tablespoons
    vegetable oil
1 cup soft brown sugar
4 eggs, lightly beaten
¼ cup light corn syrup
3¼ cups grated carrots
½ cup chopped pecans or walnuts

1. Preheat the oven to 325°F. Grease the cake pan and line the bottom and sides with a collar of waxed paper that extends ¾ inch above the top of the pan. Sift together the flours, spices, and baking soda into a large bowl and make a well in the center. Whisk together the oil, sugar, egg, and corn syrup. Gradually pour into the well, stirring until combined. Stir in the carrots and chopped nuts.

2. Spoon the mixture into the pan and smooth the surface. Bake in the oven for 1 hour 40 minutes, or until a skewer poked into the center of the cake comes out clean.

3. Leave the cake to cool in the pan for at least 15 minutes, then remove the cake and allow to cool completely on a wire rack.

Storage: Keep the cake in an airtight container in the fridge for up to 1 week, or freeze for up to 2 months.

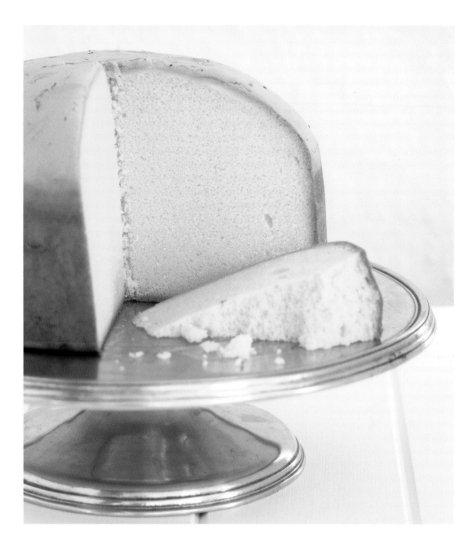

White chocolate mud cake

Makes one 9-inch round cake or
   one 8-inch square cake

½ lb plus 5 tablespoons unsalted
   butter, chopped
10½ oz white couverture chocolate,
   chopped
2 cups all-purpose flour
1 cup self-rising flour
1¾ cups superfine sugar
3 eggs, lightly beaten
1½ teaspoons natural vanilla
   extract

1. Preheat the oven to 350°F. Grease the cake pan and line the bottom and sides with a collar of waxed paper that extends ¾ inch above the top of the pan. Put the butter and 1 cup and 1 tablespoon of water in a saucepan over medium heat and stir until the butter has melted. Turn off the heat, then add the chocolate and stir until it has melted and is well combined.

2. Sift the flours together into a bowl. Add the sugar, a pinch of salt and make a well in the center.

3. Pour the chocolate mixture, egg, and vanilla into the well, then stir with a wooden spoon until well combined.

4. Pour into the cake pan. Bake for 1 hour 40 minutes, or until the cake is golden brown and a skewer comes out clean when poked into the center of the cake. Cover with foil halfway through if the cake is browning too quickly.

5. Leave to cool completely in the pan on a wire rack.

Storage: Keep the cake in an airtight container in the fridge for up to 1 week, or freeze for up to 1 month.

Coconut cake

Makes one 9-inch round cake or
   one 8-inch square cake

¾ cup plus 2½ tablespoons butter,
   softened
1¾ cups lightly packed brown
   sugar
1 teaspoon natural coconut extract
3 eggs, lightly beaten
1⅓ cups dry coconut
2⅓ cups self-rising flour
1⅓ cups plus 2 tablespoons
   buttermilk

1. Preheat the oven to 350°F. Grease the cake pan and line the bottom and sides with a collar of waxed paper that extends ¾ inch above the top of the pan.

2. Beat the butter, sugar, and coconut extract until light and fluffy. Add the eggs one at a time, beating well after each one. Fold in the combined coconut and sifted flour alternately with spoonfuls of buttermilk.

3. Spoon the mixture into the pan and smooth the surface. Bake for 1 hour 10 minutes until golden brown and a skewer poked into the center of the cake comes out clean.

4. Leave the cake in the pan for at least 5 minutes, then remove the cake and allow to cool on a wire rack.

Storage: Keep the cake in an airtight container in the fridge for 1 week, or freeze for up to 2 months.

Flourless orange and almond cake (dairy/gluten-free)

Makes one 9-inch round cake or
  one 8-inch square cake

2 to 3 oranges (with unwaxed,
  unblemished skin as the whole
  fruit is used)
8 eggs
1¾ cups superfine sugar
1 teaspoon baking powder
4¼ cups ground almonds

1. Scrub the oranges well and leave them whole. Put them in a large saucepan with enough water to cover them. Put a small plate on top of the oranges to keep them submerged. Bring to a boil, then reduce the heat, and leave to simmer gently for 1 hour until the oranges are very soft.

2. Grease the cake pan and line the bottom and sides with a collar of waxed paper that extends ¾ inch above the top of the pan.

3. Drain the oranges well, then put back into the saucepan and leave until cool enough to handle. Cut each orange into quarters, remove the seeds, then purée with a handheld blender or in a food processor.

4. Beat the eggs, sugar, baking powder, and a pinch of salt until pale and creamy. Beat in the almonds and 15 oz of the orange purée. Leave for 20 minutes and preheat the oven to 350°F.

5. Pour into the pan and bake for 1 hour 30 minutes until golden brown and a skewer poked into the center comes out clean. Cool completely in the pan.

Storage: Keep the cake in an airtight container in the fridge for up to 1 week, or freeze for up to 2 months.

Icing recipes

All the cakes in this book are first brushed with a little syrup, perfectly coated with chocolate ganache and then covered with a layer of rolled fondant icing. You'll find all these basic icing recipes in this chapter.

Ganache

The ideal chocolate for making ganache is a couverture variety with a cocoa content of 53% to 63%. In cold weather you might have to add a touch more cream or reduce the chocolate a little bit, so that the ganache isn't too hard. If you can't find couverture chocolate, try semisweet chocolate.

These recipes make approximately 4 lb of ganache, which is enough to cover each cake in this book (with a little left-over in case of mishaps).

White ganache
3 lb white chocolate, finely chopped
1¾ cups plus 1 tablespoon whipping cream

Dark ganache
2 lb 10 oz dark chocolate, finely chopped
2⅓ cups plus 1 tablespoon whipping cream

1. To make either white or dark ganache, put the chocolate pieces in a large bowl.

2. Put the cream in a saucepan and bring to a boil. Pour the cream over the chopped chocolate and mix with a hand whisk until the ganache is smooth. (Do not use an electric whisk, as you will create too many air bubbles in the ganache.)

3. Allow to cool completely and then leave to set overnight.

Microwave method

1. Put the chocolate and cream in a microwave-proof bowl and heat for 1 to 2 minutes on high, then remove and stir. Repeat heating and then stirring until the ganache is smooth.

2. Remove the bowl from the microwave, cover with plastic wrap and leave for 5 minutes. Shake the bowl a little bit so that all the chocolate sinks to the bottom.

3. Mix with a hand whisk until smooth.

4. Allow to cool completely and then leave to set overnight.

Facts about ganache

What is the difference between white and dark ganache?

The white chocolate ganache is sweeter and goes well with the coconut and carrot cake.

White chocolate ganache is less stable than dark chocolate ganache, so in hot weather, or when you are making intricate three-dimensional cakes, it is easier to use dark chocolate ganache.

What type of cream do you use to make ganache?

Always use whipping cream (no more than 36% fat) for making ganache (never "thick" or "double" cream). You should always use a cream that has a low fat content, which does not thicken when beaten.

How long does ganache keep?

You can keep ganache in the fridge usually for a week. However, always check the use-by date of your cream when you buy it and make sure it has at least one week's shelf life.

How do you store ganache?

The ganache recipe (page 31) makes enough to cover one cake, with a bit left over in case anything goes wrong. But as I make so many cakes, I like to make a big batch of ganache and then decant it into smaller containers to be frozen. If you are planning on using the ganache during the next few days, keep it in the fridge and let it come back to room temperature before using.

How do you reheat your ganache?

Ganache that is taken straight from the fridge will be too hard to spread over a cake. Keep the ganache in smaller containers and heat as much as you need in the microwave in short bursts of 10 to 20 seconds. Stir after each burst, and make sure not to "cook" your ganache or it will burn and curdle. If you don't have a microwave, put the ganache in a saucepan and heat over low heat, stirring, making sure not to burn the ganache.

Syrup

⅓ cup apricot jam
2 teaspoons orange liqueur
   (optional)

1. Whisk the jam with 6 tablespoons of boiling water until smooth.

2. Remove any lumps and stir in the orange liqueur, if using.

Rolled fondant icing

I don't make my own fondant icing as I find the commercial varieties easier and more reliable to use. But if you do need a recipe, this one is courtesy of my friend Greg Cleary — a great cake decorator.

2 tablespoons gelatin
½ cup liquid glucose
5 teaspoons glycerine
2¼ lb pure confectioners' sugar
2 drops flavor extract (optional)

1. Sprinkle the gelatin over 3 tablespoons of water in a small bowl. Leave until the gelatin is spongy.

2. Place the bowl over a saucepan of hot water and stir until the gelatin has dissolved. Add the glucose and glycerine and stir until melted. Strain through a sieve.

3. Sift the confectioners' sugar into a large bowl, make a well in the center and pour in the gelatin mixture. Mix until it becomes too difficult to stir with a spoon. Tip the mixture out onto a bench, add the flavoring, if using, and knead with dry hands into a smooth and pliable dough.

4. Wrap the icing in plastic wrap and store in an airtight container in a cool place (but do not refrigerate).

5. Knead again before using, adding more sifted confectioners' sugar as necessary.

Royal icing

Makes about 9 oz

9 to 10½ oz pure confectioners' sugar, sifted
2 to 4 drops acetic acid
1 egg white

1. Beat 9 oz of the confectioners' sugar, the acetic acid, and the egg white with electric beaters on medium–high speed for 4 minutes for a "soft peak," or over 5 minutes for "firm peak" (or beat for 20 minutes by hand). Add extra sugar if the icing is still too soft after that time.

2. "Soft peak" royal icing is used for coating cakes and icing with tubes. When lifted from the bowl with a spatula, the peak will stand up but droop over slightly at the tip.

3. Store the royal icing in an airtight container in a cool place but not in the fridge. It will keep for several days.

Note: Achieving the right consistency for royal icing can be difficult, so you may prefer to buy an instant royal icing mix where you just have to add water.

Techniques

The most important technique you'll learn in this chapter is the Planet Cake "secret" for perfectly decorated cakes: using ganache as the base for a thin layer of rolled fondant icing.

Ganaching

Chocolate ganache (a melted mixture of chocolate and cream) will not only make your cake taste better and keep it moist, but will also give you a perfect surface for icing. At Planet Cake we use ganache as a sort of edible "putty" to fill in all the crevices and holes in the cake and create an even surface to cover with rolled fondant icing.

Once the ganache has set hard and is perfectly smooth, it presents a firm and perfect surface for covering with thin icing (rather than the thick unpalatable icing that some decorators use to hide imperfections in the cake).

Follow the recipe for making ganache (page 31) and allow it to set overnight. If the ganache is too hard when you are ready to use it, heat it in short bursts in the microwave until it reaches the consistency of smooth peanut butter. If you don't have a microwave, put the ganache in a pan and heat over low heat, stirring, making sure not to burn the ganache.

Alternatively, you could use a layer of buttercream under your fondant icing but it will not set as firm as ganache and so not give you the same perfect finish.

Ganaching cupcakes

Let the cupcakes cool completely after baking, but do ganache them on the same day to prevent them drying out.

1. Syrup (optional)

Cupcakes dry out very quickly. One way to prevent this is to treat them with syrup. With a fork, or a skewer, make some holes in the top of the cupcakes and then brush fairly liberally with syrup (page 32).

2. Even out the surfaces

If your cupcakes have spilled over their paper liners or risen unevenly, cut off the tops so that they are all even. It is very difficult to ice a high-domed cupcake.

3. Spread with ganache

Using a palette knife, spread 2½ teaspoons of ganache across the top of each cupcake.

Be very careful not to smear ganache onto the paper liners, particularly if you are using semisweet chocolate ganache.

4. Hot-knife

By the time you have ganached your last cupcake your first cupcakes should be set and ready to "hot-knife". This is the way we get such a smooth finish on our ganache. To achieve a perfect result you need a jug of boiling water and a long knife. Leave the knife to stand in the hot water for a few seconds, then glide it over the surface of the ganache using even pressure. When you ganache larger cakes you hold the knife at both ends, but cupcakes are a much more manageable place to start. Let the cupcakes sit until the ganache has set hard (preferably overnight) before you start decorating them.

Ganaching a round cake

1. Slice your cake horizontally into three even layers
Trim the dome from the top of the cake to get a flat surface. Put the cake on a turntable and place one hand on top of the cake (never keep your hand on the side as the knife could slip). Hold a long serrated knife in the other hand, making sure to keep the knife level.

Mark the cutting lines on the cake by scoring the side; each layer should be about 1 inch thick. Rotate the cake and cut towards the center with a sawing action, gradually cutting deeper. Continue turning and cutting deeper every round, making sure to keep the knife at the same horizontal level.

Repeat this one more time to cut another layer.

Tip: If your cake is cracked or uneven on the top, swap the middle layer with the top layer so that you can hide it inside the cake.

2. Brush with syrup
Place the three layers of cake on your work surface and brush each fairly liberally with syrup (page 32).

3. Fill the cake with ganache
Use a palette knife to spread some ganache on a cake board the same size as the cake; for example, an 8-inch cake would be placed on an 8-inch board. We refer to this board as the set-up or DIY board.

Apply ganache to each layer of the cake to about ½ inch thick and sandwich the layers together.

Tip: Having a set-up or DIY board is very important when ganaching as it allows you to make a big mess and, most importantly, serves as a guide for measuring the filling. Cakes shrink during the baking process and

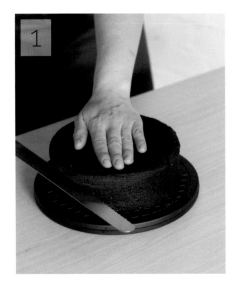

by placing the cake on the same size cake board you can see how much ganache to apply to bring the cake back to the correct size.

4. Apply ganache to the side
With a palette knife, apply ganache all around the side of the cake out to the edge of the set-up or DIY board. Do not put ganache on the top of the cake at this point.

5. Scrape off the excess ganache
Using the turntable, put one hand on the top of the cake and run the plastic scraper slowly around the side of the cake. Make sure to hold the scraper straight on the edge of the board and continue turning until your cake has a perfectly vertical edge and all the gaps are filled.

Tip: Your goal is to fill the side of the cake until it meets the rim of the set-up or DIY board. This may take some time and will require more ganache than you envisage. Make sure you have a perfect right angle — if the filling bulges out there will be a lump on your cake. Alternatively, if there is not enough ganache and the side is not flat you will have ridges.

6. Apply ganache to the top
Use a small palette knife to smear the excess ganache over the edge of the cake and onto the top, then level the top. Use more ganache on the top if necessary. Let the ganache set on the cake (preferably overnight) or freeze for a maximum of 10 minutes.

7. Hot-knife
To achieve a perfect result you will need a jug of boiling water and a long knife to run over the cake to make sure the edge is perfect. Take a large palette knife, or the back of a bread knife, and leave it to stand in

the hot water for a few seconds. Hold the knife at both ends and glide it over the surface of the cake, making sure to apply even pressure along the whole length of the knife. If the ganache is uneven, apply more to level the cake.

Run the plastic scraper once more around the side of the cake. Let the cake set again and, when it is hard, use a hot knife to cut the overhang off the top edge. Clean your board and leave the cake until the ganache has set hard (preferably overnight) before you cover it.

Ganaching a square cake

Follow the same guidelines as for the round cake until Step 4.

The same method applies to rectangular cakes.

1. Ganache and smooth

Apply the ganache thickly to the sides (about ¾ inch) with a palette knife to build up the cake. Scrape off the excess with a scraper and apply more ganache until you have very sharp edges. Smooth the ganache, then let it set (for 1 to 2 hours) until it is firm to the touch. Apply ganache on the top, smooth and let it set (preferably overnight).

2. Hot-knife

Hot-knife the ganache starting at one side and then glide over the surface, making sure to apply even pressure along the length of the knife. Scrape off any excess ganache. Run the plastic scraper once more along the sides and take special care to keep the corners sharp.

Cutting and ganaching a rectangular cake

All the recipes for shaped cakes call for rectangular cakes. This is how to shape an 8-inch square cake into a 12 x 8 inch rectangular cake and then ganache it.

1. Slice the cake into layers

Place an 8-inch square cake on a clean work surface, or turntable, and cut the dome from the top of the cake to get a leveled surface. Place one hand on top of the cake (never keep your hand on the side as the knife could slip). Hold a long serrated knife in the other hand, making sure to keep the knife level, then slice the cake twice horizontally to make three even layers.

Spread out the three layers and brush each one with syrup (page 32). Cut one layer in half to 8 x 4 inches.

2. Make and fill a rectangle

Take one of the half layers and sandwich it on one normal layer with ganache. Put the other normal and half layer on top and sandwich them together with ganache. Trim the sides and place the cake on a set-up or DIY board of 12 x 8 inches.

3. Apply ganache to the sides and top

Put the cake on a turntable. Apply a little bit of ganache on the cake to seal the crumbs, then apply more ganache around the sides with a palette knife, until you get a rectangle of 12 x 8 inches. Slowly run the scraper along the sides, making sure you are holding it straight on the board and at a right angle. Use a small palette knife to smooth the excess ganache from the sides up over the edges and onto the top. Even the top, using more ganache if necessary (see ganaching a square cake, page 39).

Let the ganache set on the cake (preferably overnight). To speed up the process you can freeze the cake for a maximum of 10 minutes until the ganache is firm to the touch.

4. Hot-knife

To achieve a perfect result you will need a jug of boiling water and a long knife to run over the cake to make sure the edges are perfect. Take a large palette knife, or the back of a bread knife, and leave it to stand in the water for a few seconds. Hold the knife at both ends and

glide it over the surface of the cake, making sure to apply even pressure along the length of the knife. If the ganache is uneven, apply more to level the cake.

5. Perfecting the edges

Run your plastic scraper along the sides of the cake. Let the cake set hard for several hours or preferably overnight. When it is set hard, use a sharp knife to cut the overhang off the top edge.

Cutting and ganaching a shaped cake

After you have shaped your square cake into a rectangle, and before you ganache the sides, you need to make a template from cardboard that will also act as a DIY board (page 62).

1. Build up the cake
Place the template/DIY board on top of your cake and, using a sharp knife held at a right angle, cut around it. If the cake is not large enough, use the trim-offs to build up your shape, using ganache as edible glue.

2. Cut into shape
Cut around the template/DIY board at a right angle to make the shape.

3. Place cake on DIY board
Put the shaped cake on the DIY board. Roughly ganache the finished shape and let the ganache set. Hot-knife it, and then let it set again.

Cutting and ganaching a three-dimensional cake

These cakes always need to be cut into two or three even layers and filled with ganache to achieve a certain height and stability. Put the cake onto a set-up or DIY board. Let the ganache set so the cake will be firm and easier to work with.

1. Build up the cake
To create the required shape, use the trim-offs from the cake and stick them together with ganache. Press them firmly into shape and stick the pressed pieces onto the cake.

Use your hands to mold and press the cake pieces together until you have the required shape.

2. Cut into shape
Using a serrated knife and with a sawing action, cut off excess cake and trim into shape. Let the cake rest for 1 to 2 hours. Ganache the whole cake, smooth and let it set. Ganache and let it set again, then hot-knife it.

Using rolled fondant (or ready-to-use) icing

Rolled fondant icing dries very quickly so you need to work fast to avoid it becoming cracked and difficult to use. Always work with small amounts of icing. Keep the icing you are not working with in a plastic bag or cover it with a plastic sheet to prevent it drying out.

The weather will affect your fondant icing: humidity will make the icing sticky and very cold weather will make it as hard as rock. I sometimes wait a day if it is bad "fondant" weather!

Cool your hands in cold water before you knead icing and use only a light sprinkling of cornstarch. When kneading your icing on a bench, it is a good idea to lean over the icing so you can use your body weight to help you knead. Never cover a cake that you have taken straight from the fridge as it will sweat underneath the icing. To achieve a professional finish let your cake come to room temperature first.

Never use icing that is too dry, or that has been over-kneaded, or you will find that the corners will crack very easily. When you are making dark colors that require a lot of food color such as red, black, brown, or purple, color the icing a day in advance so it has time to relax and rest.

Once you have covered your cake, do not refrigerate it as the icing will sweat and become soggy. Store your decorated cake in a cool dry place (up to 68°F).

Any left-over fondant icing is best stored in a sealed plastic bag or an airtight container. You should follow the manufacturer's instructions on how to store your particular brand of icing. I store my icing at room temperature.

Covering cupcakes

1. Roll the icing and cut out circles
Roll out the icing to ⅛ inch thick using a pasta machine or rolling pin. Cut out circles with a round cutter in the closest size to your cupcakes. Keep the icing discs covered with a plastic sheet to prevent them drying out.

2. Smooth the icing
Brush each cupcake with syrup (page 32) and stick the icing disc on top. Push the icing into place until it sits perfectly on the surface of the cupcake, and then use a flexi-scraper to smooth the icing.

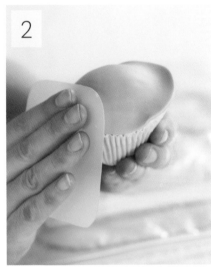

Covering a round cake

Make sure your cake is smoothly ganached and allowed to set before you cover it with icing. The more perfectly the cake is ganached, the better the final result will be.

1. Prepare the cake

Wipe down your work surface clean and make sure it is dry. Measure the cake (side and top surface). Brush the cake all over with a little syrup (page 32); this helps the fondant stick to the cake.

Stick your cake onto a set-up board, or onto its display board, with a bit of royal icing and place the board on a nonslip mat, so that is does not slip while you are working on it.

2. Flatten and roll the icing

Make sure your icing is smooth. Flatten your ball of icing first with the palm of your hand to about 1½-inch thickness before rolling it with the rolling pin (this makes it easier to roll). Knead the icing to a pliable dough using a sprinkle of cornstarch if it sticks.

Lightly dust your work surface with cornstarch. Roll the icing, starting from the center rolling about six times in one direction.

Turn the icing and repeat the process. If your work surface gets sticky use a bit more cornstarch, but never use cornstarch on top of the icing! The turning of the icing will ensure that the icing will always be a square, which will make covering a round or square cake much easier.

Keep on rolling and turning until your icing is about ⅛ inch thick; the icing needs to be larger than the total cake measurement.

Note: Kneading icing is not like kneading dough. If you keep pummelling it, it will stick to the board and become unmanageable. Treat your icing a bit like "play dough": keep folding it in until it is smooth and warm to use but doesn't stick.

3. Lift the icing over the cake

Pick up the icing by rolling it onto the rolling pin. Use a dry pastry brush to remove any excess cornstarch (this is particularly important if you use dark-colored icing).

Lift the rolling pin with the icing up and unroll it over the cake starting from the bottom of the cake.

4. Secure the edges

Quickly run your hand over the top surface to make sure there are no air bubbles. Secure the edges by running the palms of your hands along the top edge and side of the cake.

5. Smooth the icing

Press the icing gently on the side, working around the cake. Pull the icing away from the side of the cake before smoothing it down.

6. Use icing smoothers

Once the whole cake is covered, gently press the icing against the side and base of the cake using icing smoothers.

7. Trim the icing

Trim the icing around the base with a pizza wheel or a knife.

Tip: Do not trim your icing too close to the bottom of your cake, as the icing shrinks and you could be left with a gap. If this does happen, adjust your design and place a roll around the base of the cake (page 62).

8. Use your smoothers

Run your smoothers along the side of the cake. I use two smoothers to do this job; the one in the left hand is running back and forth and the one in the right hand is pressed against the cake to make a sharp edge. Hold one smoother on the side of the cake and the other one on the top surface. Using the same amount of pressure, press them together and run along the side of the cake to give a sharp edge.

Glide your hand along the cake feeling for air bubbles. If there are any, poke a small pin into the bubble and gently release the air with your dry fingers (page 65).

Go over the cake with your smoother or flexi-scraper to buff and polish the icing.

Covering a square cake

Follow the same guidelines as for the round cake until Step 3 (page 44).

Once the cake is covered, quickly secure the surface by running your hands along the top, smoothing and pressing the icing.

1. Secure the corners
Secure the corners immediately by running your hands towards the corner and pressing the icing onto the cake.

2. Push the icing down
Push the icing right down the corners with your fingers by running up and down along the edges.

3. Pull and smooth the sides
Gently pull the icing away from the sides with one hand and smooth it down with the other hand. Then run your hands up again to avoid tears or cracks in the icing. Trim the icing all around the bottom using a small knife or pizza wheel.

4. Smooth the icing
Use two flexi-scrapers and run them towards each other at the corners to achieve a sharp edge.

Covering shaped cakes

Covering a shaped cake will always be different depending on the design. Therefore, feel your ganached cake with your hands, getting to know each crease and turn and also remove any crumbs or sharp edges, before you start icing your cake.

1. Secure the edges and smooth the icing
Secure the edges and all creases with your hands and fingers. Smooth the icing by gently pulling the icing away from the side before smoothing it down with your hand.

2. Trim the icing
Cut away the overhanging icing with scissors. Smooth the joining line with your fingers or a flexi-scraper. Trim the icing around the bottom with a small knife or pizza wheel.

3. Polish the icing
Using your flexi-scraper, buff and polish the icing against the shape of the cake, creating a more defined shape. Gently work the cake with your hands and flexi-scraper making sure you eliminate any air bubbles.

4. Secure edges
Cover the dome with icing. Secure the edge and smooth the icing with your hands.

5. Cut off excess icing
Mark a cutting line around the cake first, then cut off the excess icing with a small knife.

6. Apply icing sideways
Roll your icing onto a small rolling pin and unroll the icing around the cake, like unrolling a carpet.

Covering a board with icing

There are two methods of covering a cake board: to cover the whole board, or just to cover the part that is visible around the cake. And it isn't necessary to cover your board at all — in fact many decorators don't. I cover my boards because I like the clean finish it gives (and I also personally don't like the look of silver or gold boards, which can undermine the effect of the cake).

Covering the whole board

1. Roll out the icing
Roll out the icing to ⅛ inch thick and at least the same size as the board. Place the icing on the board. If it is too small, keep on rolling it directly on the board until it covers the whole surface.

2. Make the icing stick
Dip a pastry brush in some water, lift the icing halfway up and brush the board. Lay the icing down and do the same to the other side.

3. Trim the icing
Use a flexi-scraper, or an acrylic smoother, and go over the surface to create a neat finish. Trim away most of the excess icing with scissors. Place the iced board on a turntable, or halfway over the table, and, using the acrylic smoother, hold it at a 45° angle and slide along the edge to cut the icing. This will give you a nice bevelled edge.

4. Place the cake on the board
Let the icing on the board dry, then stick the cake onto it with a dab of royal icing (page 33) to keep the cake on the set-up or DIY board.

Tip: If you choose to use this method to cover your board it is essential that your cake sits on a set-up or DIY board. For round and square cakes you can use ready-made boards as set-up boards. For shaped cakes you will need to make your own DIY board from waxed cardboard (page 62).

Covering a board around the cake

For round and square cakes

Prepare and cover the cake on the final display board (pages 44–46).

1. Roll the icing and use a cake board as a template

Roll out the icing to about ⅛ inch thick and at least the same size as as the final display board. Place a cake board in the exact same size as the cake, or a little smaller, in the center of the rolled icing and cut it out using a small paring knife.

Tip: I always cut the template a bit smaller than the size of the cake, because when you lift the icing it will automatically stretch slightly.

2. Place the icing

Lift the icing carefully over the cake, and push and manipulate the icing to fit snugly around the cake.

3. Make the icing stick to the board

Trim some of the excess icing with scissors. Lift the icing up and brush a bit of water on the board.

4. Smooth the icing

Stick the icing down and use a flexi-scraper to smooth it out. Use an acrylic smoother to cut the icing on a 45° angle to the board.

Tip: For a perfect finish, place a thin ribbon around the board. Place the board on a turntable and stick the ribbon around the edge by using glue. Make sure the ribbon joins at the back of your cake.

Covering a board around the cake

For shaped cakes

Prepare and cover the cake on the final display board (page 47).

1. Roll the icing and use a DIY template

Roll out the icing to about ⅛ inch thick and at least the same size as the final display board. Use the template of your cake and cut the icing around it. Use a clean paring knife to do this. It is particularly important to use a template for the shaped cakes. However, for rounds or squares we just use a cake board.

2. Place the icing

Cut a slit in the icing at the back to allow access for the cake. Like placing a horseshoe, place the icing on the board and around the cake, making sure the slit is at the back.

3.+4. Manipulate and trim the icing

To make sure the icing meets at the back for a perfect join, let the icing overlap a little. Then trim to make the edges of the icing meet perfectly. Push and manipulate the icing to fit snugly around the cake.

5. Make the icing stick

Lift the icing up and brush a bit of water on the board. Stick the icing down and with a flexi-scraper smooth it out.

6. Trim the icing

Use an acrylic smoother to cut the icing on a 45° angle to the board.

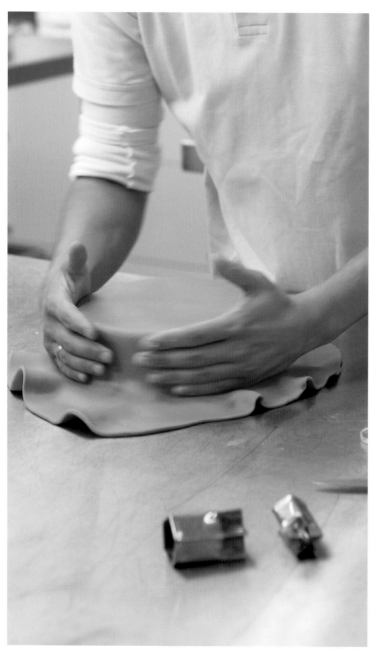

Techniques, tips and troubleshooting

When you are starting off, making a bow, or a tassel, or even a perfect layer of thinly rolled icing can seem daunting. Follow these step-by-step instructions and you will see how easy it all is. And, however experienced and wonderful a decorator you become, occasionally things will go wrong. That doesn't mean you have to start again — our troubleshooting guide will show you how to deal with the common problems that occur.

Coloring icing

1. Measure the color
Knead the icing to a pliable dough. Add only a tiny amount of food coloring at a time.

2. Add the color
Smear the color onto the icing, then knead until it is evenly distributed. Wear gloves to prevent staining your hands.

3.+4. Check the color
Cut through your icing to check if the color is evenly blended. If there are still swirls of color, keep kneading, and checking, until the color is solid all the way through. Or, leave the color as it is for a marbled effect in your icing.

Tip: When you want to color your icing very strongly, making deep colors such as black, brown, red, purple, or royal blue, it is better to use paste food coloring. Since you need much more color, a liquid color would make the icing too sticky to work with. Even if you are using paste, color your icing a day in advance as it will be exceptionally soft due to the large amount of color pigment.

Fading: Some colors are more prone to fading than others. Pink shades are susceptible to fading out quickly when exposed to sunlight. Pink and mauve can be reduced to almost white, purples to blues, blues to gray, and black to purple or green. Avoid the problem by either covering your cake with a clean cloth, or keeping it in a cake box.

Using a pasta machine to roll icing

1. Roll out the icing first with a rolling pin

Work out which setting on your pasta machine will roll pasta (or icing) to ⅛ inch thick. This is the usual thickness we use for covering most cakes. Knead and roll out the icing first with a small rolling pin.

2. Run the icing through the pasta machine

Feed your piece of icing through the pasta machine, and keep feeding it through until it reaches a ⅛ inch thickness, just as you would a piece of pasta.

Glazing icing

For glazing icing you can either use jam diluted with boiling water (strain to remove any lumps), or olive oil cooking spray. Apply the glaze with a paintbrush as close as possible to the time you are serving the cake. There is also a professional product (you can buy this from cake supply shops) which is a clear gel for glazing tortes and fruits.

Sticking icing

Icing is made from sugar and so will "stick" to itself with the addition of water alone. You can use syrup (page 32) instead of water, if you prefer. Paint a very faint line of water on the icing and stick the other icing piece onto it. Don't apply too much water or the icing will become soggy. To stick icing onto aquarium tubing or acetate, use piping gel.

Making a tassel

Method one

1. Roll the icing through the pasta machine

Roll out the icing to ⅛ inch thick in the pasta machine. Then use the spaghetti setting on the pasta machine and roll the icing through it to make thin lengths.

2. Fold the icing threads over to make a tassel

Fold your "spaghetti" over and pinch together at the top. "Tie" with a thin piece of icing rope. Finish the tassel with a twisted icing rope, made from two icing rolls twisted together to look like tassel cord.

Method two

1. Make a tassel with a knife

Shape a rectangular block of icing of about ½ inch thick. Slice it thinly with a knife, pinching it at the top and creating a thin rope of icing near the top.

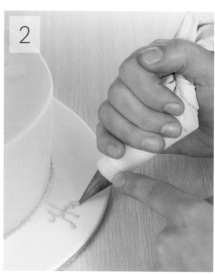

Decorating with royal icing

Tip: The round icing tips used for royal icing come in an assortment of sizes (no. 00 to 12) and the numbers correspond with the size of the hole, no. 00 being the smallest.

No. 1 icing tip and smaller could be frustrating for new decorators, so it is better to start with a no. 2 tip or bigger and gradually work to fine decorating. If you are only decorating with royal icing and not with buttercream, you will only need a couple of round icing tips to start.

Making royal icing: You can make your royal icing from scratch (recipe page 33) or buy instant royal icing mix, which is a good substitute. Before decorating with royal icing, it is essential to have it at the correct consistency: not too runny, and not too thick as it will keep blocking the icing tip.

Tip: Royal icing dries to a very hard consistency and it will begin setting as soon as it is made, so always keep it covered with plastic wrap.

Color: If you wish to color your royal icing, add food coloring in very small quantities and mix the royal icing and color together using a palette knife. You can do this on a board or plate. Don't make the color too dark as it will darken when it dries.

Equipment: Disposable plastic and cloth icing bags are perfect for home decorating. If you have a cloth bag like the one pictured in our equipment chapter (page 15), you will need a coupler as well as an icing tip.

1. Fill the bag
Only fill the icing bag one-third full with royal icing and push the icing down towards the tip end of the bag. Give it a few squeezes to get rid of the air pockets. If you find it difficult to hold the bag and fill it at the same time, you can place the bag in a glass to support it while you fill it.

2. Decorating
Practice some lines before you start decorating on the cake. Fit the icing bag with a plain icing tip in the size you desire. Hold the bag correctly with two hands, one hand to guide and the other to squeeze the bag. Hold the icing bag at a 45° angle just above the work surface. Apply pressure and see the icing emerge from the tip. Secure the end of the icing thread to the surface, then decorate, allowing the thread to fall into position.

Tip: Start with simple designs and practice until you feel confident. To create board messages you need to learn a "font."

Tracing letters and applying edible glitter

1. Trace onto waxed (or parchment) paper
Trace your desired image or font onto waxed paper using a 2B pencil. Fold the waxed paper over and trace the back of the same image.

2. Place it on the cake
Place the template right-side up on the cake and, by lightly shading your waxed paper, transfer the image onto the cake.

3. Apply piping gel
Use a fine paintbrush to apply piping gel to your traced image.

4. Dust with edible glitter
Dust the wet area with edible glitter and allow it to dry.

5. Brush away excess glitter
Dust away the excess glitter with a soft brush.

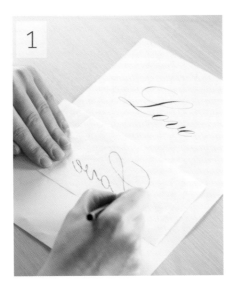

Making a bow

1. Roll the icing
Roll out the icing to ⅛ inch thick with a rolling pin or in a pasta machine. Cut two rectangles of 15 x 10 inches. Cover the icing you are not working on with a plastic sheet, so that it doesn't dry out and crack. With a small paintbrush, lightly brush along the two short sides of the rectangle with water.

2. Pleat the icing
Pinch pleats on both short sides of the rectangle simultaneously.

3. Use absorbent cotton as filling
Put absorbent cotton in the center of the rectangle. Remove when the icing has dried.

4. Fold the icing over
Fold one side over to bring both pleated sides together and gently press the ends together.

5. Sit the bow loop up
Lift the bow loop up (as it would sit on the cake) and fold one side underneath. You should now have half a bow. Place the folded side on a board and repeat the same process with the other icing rectangle.

6. Trim the ends
Trim the center a little and push the bow loops together.

7. Make the bow knot
Roll out your left-over icing to ⅛ inch thick. Cut a small rectangle of white icing to about 3¼ x 4 inches. Fold the short side into pleats to get the bow knot.

8. Assemble the bow
Place the bow knot over the ends of the bow loops, pinch the edges together. Trim at the back.

Making a zipper

1. Mark the icing

Roll out the icing to about ⅛ inch thick and cut it into a rectangle to the length you require. Cut out two strips, one ¼ inch wide and the other 1 inch wide. Cover the icing with a plastic sheet to prevent it drying out.

Run a serrated dough wheel along the center of the thin strip to mark the zipper teeth. Use your ruler and stitching tool to mark a line on both edges of the wider strip. Stick the thinner strip of icing on top of the wider strip.

2. Paint the zipper

Mix decorating alcohol and edible gold dust and paint the zipper using a fine paintbrush.

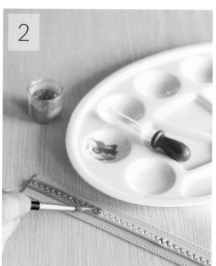

Covering acetate film

Acetate film is a flexible plastic used in stationery or computer laser printing. It is also a good "frame" for creating cake decorations, such as flip flop straps, as you can insert the film into the icing or cake and it will be invisible and light.

1. Brush the acetate with piping gel

Apply the piping gel with a brush onto your strip of acetate.

2. Place the icing on the acetate

Place a strip of icing on either side. Trim the excess and smooth down any fuzzy bits with a damp finger. You can either cover the film before or after it is inserted into the cake. If covering beforehand, leave the area to be inserted into the cake without icing and cover any unsightly joins.

Note: Remember to advise those eating the cake that this decoration is inedible.

Making sand icing

1. Mix and color the sand
Mix 5½ oz royal icing and ⅓ cup of raw sugar together. Add one drop of coral brown food coloring at a time until you get a sand color.

2. Apply with a palette knife
Apply the sand icing with a palette knife to your board or cake immediately as it will start drying quickly and become rock hard.

Making coals

Roll out a piece of dark gray icing to ¼ inch thick. Place pieces of orange, red, and black icing on the gray icing in a random pattern. Carefully roll over with a rolling pin to about ⅛ inch thick.

Frilling

Roll a small piece of icing into a rectangle of 1/16 inch thickness. Firmly roll the frilling tool back and forth using your other hand to catch the icing as it bunches. To create a long frill (required for the Princess cake, page 105) do short strips of frilling and join them together on the cake with a dab of water.

Basic painting

Mix a small amount of food coloring with decorating alcohol and paint a test piece of icing first. Work quickly, as the "paint" dries almost instantly. Work with small quantities at a time.

Tip: The silver and gold dust can spread everywhere. To prevent this, cover unpainted areas on your cake with paper.

Making an icing roll

1. Roll the icing with your hands
Using your hands, roll the icing to the basic shape of a rope.

2. Roll even with a smoother
Using an icing smoother, roll the rope back and forth, pulling it slightly out to the sides to elongate it. If the icing begins to slip under the smoother and does not roll easily, use your paintbrush to paint a thin line of water right next to and parallel with the rope, then use the smoother to roll the icing across the water. This will make the icing a little bit stickier, which will help it "catch" and roll easily underneath the smoother. Continue to roll and stretch the icing rope until it is the desired width and length.

Marking a paper cupcake liner

Make the indentations for the "paper liner" using a wooden dowel. You can also use a barbecue skewer or a chopstick.

Making a template and a DIY board

Enlarge and trace one of the templates from this book onto waxed paper and cut out to create the DIY template. Place it on top of waxed cardboard and cut around it to create the DIY board. Put the DIY board under the cake so you can move it around more easily.

Mending torn icing

1. Gap in icing
Tearing is usually the result of smoothing and pulling your icing down too vigorously when covering.

2. Smooth the tear
While the icing is still soft, use your hands and a flexi-scraper and massage the icing up and around the tear so that the tear gap is closed and almost invisible. If you are still left with a hole, wait until the icing has dried (next day). Make a small ball of fresh icing in the same color as the bottom and massage the fresh icing into the tear like putty. Smooth with a flexi-scraper and allow to dry.

Covering up cracked icing

Cracks usually appear on corners or edges when the icing is too dry. A huge crack is impossible to fix, but you can cover it up with some decorations such as icing flowers so nobody will notice it.

Mending cracked icing

While your icing is still soft, use very warm hands and massage the icing inwards around the cracks, closing them and rendering them until almost invisible.

Cleaning stained icing

Cornstarch stain

1. Apply decorating alcohol
Apply decorating alcohol with a soft paintbrush on the stain. The alcohol will absorb the cornstarch.

2. Pat dry
Pat the spot dry with a soft tissue.

Chocolate stain

1. Wash with soapy water
Use a soft paintbrush and wash the stain lightly with a very small amount of warm soapy water.

2. Dust with cornflour
Rinse your brush and wash the soap away with clean water. Lightly dry with a tissue and then use a soft brush to lightly dust with cornstarch.

Humidity

Due to humidity, icing often becomes soft and sticky. To solve this, mix sifted confectioners' sugar into the icing a little at a time and knead it through.

Icing too dry

If your icing is dry and cracking, apply a little water to it, using a brush, then knead it through. Alternatively, brush the icing with a small amount of glycerine (see glossary, page 17) and knead it through.

Icing too wet

Wet icing is usually the result of too much color pigment. Therefore black, red, and brown icing often become "wet" and difficult to work with. To solve this, knead sifted confectioners' sugar into your icing a little at a time, until it becomes less sticky but is still pliable.

Air bubbles

Feel over your cake for air bubbles, then lightly prick any with a pin to let the air escape, then smooth over your icing with a flexi-scraper. Always try to eliminate air bubbles under your icing as they will get bigger and lift the icing.

Cupcakes

I have yet to discover anyone who doesn't love cupcakes, so what better (or easier) place to start? These make a great introduction to the equipment and techniques needed for decorating larger cakes, such as using ganache, and coloring and handling the icing.

All cupcake designs by Anna Maria Roche.

Bow cupcakes

Material
12 cupcakes
7 tablespoons syrup
9 oz ganache
1 lb 2 oz pink icing (cupcakes)
1 lb 2 oz black icing (bows)
Cornstarch

Equipment
Skewer
Pastry brush
Cranked palette knife
Large and small rolling pins
Pasta machine
Plastic sheets
Flexi-scraper
Set of circle cutters
Cornstarch
Small kitchen knife or paring knife
Paintbrush

Syrup the cupcakes
Follow the instructions on how to syrup cupcakes (page 37).

Ganache the cupcakes
Follow the instructions on how to ganache cupcakes (page 37).

Cover the cupcakes
Knead the pink icing to a pliable dough and roll out to ⅛ inch thick. Using a circle cutter in the same size as the cupcakes, cut out 12 circles and stick them onto the cupcakes (page 43).

Make the ribbon strip
Roll out 7 oz of the black icing to ⅛ inch thick (be careful not to get cornstarch on top of the icing). Cut strips of ½ inch wide and slightly longer than the width of the cupcake. Cover with plastic to prevent drying.

Mark a line of water across the center of each cupcake and place the ribbon strip. Trim the ends with a sharp knife so that the strip sits flush with the cupcake (step 1).

Make the bow loops
Roll out 10½ oz of the black icing (be careful not to get any cornstarch on top of the icing). Cut two ½-inch wide strips, one strip about 4 inches long and then a shorter strip. Fold the ends of the longer strip over to make bow loops, and stick in place with a dab of water. Cover the center with the shorter strip, making a faux knot (steps 2+3) and attach to the ribbon strip with a dab of water (step 3).

Tip: Insert tissue paper in the loops and remove when the icing has dried.

Glaze (optional): Follow the instructions on how to glaze (page 54). Glaze the ribbon and bow.

1. Place a strip of black icing across the middle of each cupcake to make the ribbon and trim the ends. 2. Fold the ends of the longer strip over and glue in place with a dab of water. Cover the center with the shorter strip to make a knot. 3. Attach the bow to the ribbon strip with a dab of water.

Dragonfly cupcakes

Material
12 cupcakes
7 tablespoons syrup
9 oz ganache
1 lb 2 oz purple icing (cupcakes)
9 oz white icing (wings)
9 oz deep purple icing (dragonfly)
Florist wire or mung bean noodles
Cornstarch

Equipment
Skewer
Pastry brush
Cranked palette knife
Large and small rolling pins
Pasta machine
Plastic sheets
Set of circle cutters
Flexi-scraper
Plastic scraper
Heart cutter
Paintbrush
Small kitchen knife or paring knife

1
2
3
4

1. Cover the cupcakes. 2. Cut the wings using a heart cutter and then cut them in half.
3. Apply the body of the dragonfly in a curved line. 4. Attach the wings and add the antennae.

Syrup the cupcakes
Follow the instructions on how to syrup cupcakes (page 37).

Ganache the cupcakes
Follow the instructions on how to ganache cupcakes (page 37).

Cover the cupcakes
Knead the purple icing to a pliable dough and roll out to 1/8 inch thick. Using a circle cutter in the same size as the cupcakes, cut out 12 circles and stick them onto the cupcakes (page 43), (step 1).

Make the wings
Roll out the white icing in a pasta machine (page 54), or by hand, and cut two hearts per cupcake with the heart cutter, then cut them in half (step 2).

Make the body
Use the deep purple icing to roll seven to eight balls per cupcake graduating in size from a baby pea to a large pea.
Paint a curved line of water on the cupcake and stick the balls on the icing starting from the largest size (step 3). Attach the wings (step 4).

Make the antennae
Use two small pieces of mung bean noodles or thin wire per cupcake as antennae. Roll two tiny balls of white icing and stick them on the ends of the noodles.

Note: When making the cupcakes for children, use mung bean noodles for the antennae as they are edible.

71

These sweet little baby cupcakes make the perfect gift for a baby shower. If you don't know whether the baby's going to be a boy or a girl, just use a mix of pastel colors for the beanies and pacifiers. For a first birthday party, you could even pipe the baby's name onto the beanies.

Baby cupcakes with beanies and pacifiers

Material
12 cupcakes
7 tablespoons syrup
9 oz ganache
1 lb 2 oz skin-colored icing (mix red, orange, and brown) (cupcakes)
Red petal dust
Cornstarch
1¾ oz white icing (eyes)
1¾ oz black icing (eyes)
7 oz light blue icing (beanies)
9 oz pink icing (pacifiers)
9 oz yellow icing (quiffs)

Equipment
Skewer
Pastry brush
Cranked palette knife
Large and small rolling pins
Pasta machine
Plastic sheets
Set of circle cutters
Flexi-scraper
No. 2 icing tip
Paintbrushes
Frilling tool
Clear plastic drinking straw

Syrup the cupcakes
Follow the instructions on how to syrup cupcakes (page 37).

Ganache the cupcakes
Follow the instructions on how to ganache cupcakes (page 37).

Cover the cupcakes
Knead the skin-colored icing to a pliable dough and roll out to ⅛ inch thick. Using a circle cutter in the same size as the cupcakes, cut out 12 circles and stick them onto the cupcakes (page 43).

1

2

3

3

4

5

6

1. Use the frilling tool to make the indents for the eyes.

2. Use the circle cutter to cut out the beanies and then cut in half. Add the trim and pompom.

3. Attach the eyes.

4. Make the pacifiers.

5. Make the hair quiff and bow.

6. Attach the dummy, hair quiff and bow.

For rosy cheeks, mix red petal dust with cornstarch (to dilute) and dust on the face with a dry paintbrush.

Make the nose and ears
Roll a small ball of skin-colored icing for the nose and stick it in the center of the face with a little water. With the frilling tool, mark two holes for the eyes. Make two balls from skin-colored icing for the ears and stick them on either side of the face, level with the nose. Press the frilling tool into each ball to give them an ear shape (step 1).

Make the mouth
While the icing is still soft, use the edge of a round cutter to indent the mouth on the babies that will not have a dummy (step 2).

Finish the eyes
Roll out tiny balls of white icing and stick them into the indents. Using tiny amount of black icing, roll out even smaller balls and stick them on top of the white balls (step 3).

Make the beanie
Roll out the light blue icing to ⅛ inch thick. Cut out circles, using the same size circle cutter you used for the cupcake. Cut off one-third with the same cutter, then stick the beanies on the cupcakes. Roll a piece of the light blue icing into a small ball and stick it onto the beanie to make a pompom. Re-roll the light blue icing out to ⅛ inch thick, cut a thin strip and stick it on the beanie's rim. Trim and decorate (step 2).

Make the dummy
Roll out the blue icing to about ¼ inch thick and cut out a circle of ¾ inch with an icing tip. Make a roll of pink icing and cut it to a ¼ inch cylinder. Stick the cylinder onto the circle with a little water (step 4). Stick the pacifiers in the cupcakes without noses, with a little water (step 6).

Make the hair quiff and bow
For the quiff, roll a small amount of yellow icing into a cone, twist the cone and stick it to the head with a little water (steps 5+6).

For the bow, roll blue icing out to ⅛ inch, and cut two strips, one three times longer than the other. Fold the long strip inwards to the center for the bow loops. Fix the short strip on the center for the bow knot. Stick the bow on the hair quiff with a little water (steps 5+6).

Honeybee cupcakes

Material
2¼ oz white icing (wings)
12 cupcakes
7 tablespoons syrup
9 oz ganache
1 lb 2 oz chocolate brown icing (cupcakes)
9 oz yellow icing (stripes)
1¾ oz black icing (stinger)
¾ oz white icing (eyes)
¾ oz black icing (eyes)
Mung bean noodles
¾ oz yellow icing (antennae)
Cornstarch

Equipment
Skewer
Pastry brush
Cranked palette knife
Large and small rolling pins
Pasta machine
Heart cutter
Set of circle cutters
Flexi-scraper
Small kitchen knife or paring knife
Frilling tool
Paintbrushes
Plastic drinking straw

1. Trim the yellow stripes and make two indents for the eyeholes. 2. Make the antennae and the stinger. 3. Stick white dots of icing into the indents for the eyes and make the wings. Attach the antennae and stinger. 4. Finish the eyes and apply the wings.

Make the wings
Knead a small amount of white icing and roll out to ⅛ inch thick. Cut out hearts with a heart cutter, then cut in half and trim the point. Gently curl the wings over a pen. Let it dry for at least a day.

Syrup the cupcakes
Follow the instructions on how to syrup cupcakes (page 37).

Ganache the cupcakes
Follow the instructions on how to ganache cupcakes (page 37).

Cover the cupcakes
Knead the chocolate brown icing to a pliable dough and roll out to ⅛ inch thick. Using a circle cutter the same size as the cupcakes, cut out 12 circles and stick them onto the cupcakes (page 43).

Make the stripes
Roll out the yellow icing to ⅛ inch thick. Cut three to four 4 x ½ inch strips for each cupcake. Stick the strips onto the cupcake with a dab of water. Trim the edges with a sharp knife (step 1).

Make the antennae and stinger
Use two ⅝ inch long mung bean noodles for the antennas. Roll two tiny balls of yellow icing and stick

them on the ends of the noodles (steps 2+3). Shape a small cone from the black icing and stick it on with a little water (steps 2+3).

Make the face
Use a frilling tool to indent two holes for the eyes (step 1). Cut a drinking straw in half to mark the mouth. Roll out tiny balls of white icing and stick them into the indents. Using tiny amount of black icing, roll out even smaller balls and stick them on top of the white balls (steps 3+4). Poke in the antennae.

Place the wings
Pipe a small amount of white royal icing on the center of the bee and stick on the dried wings.

Green monster cupcakes

Material
12 cupcakes
7 tablespoons syrup
9 oz ganache
1 lb 2 oz black icing (cupcakes)
10½ oz green icing (face)
9 oz white icing (eyes and teeth)
1¾ oz orange icing (eyes)
3½ oz red icing (lips)
Cornstarch

Equipment
Skewer
Pastry brush
Cranked palette knife
Large and small rolling pins
Pasta machine
Plastic sheets
Set of circle cutters
Flexi-scraper
Small kitchen knife
Frilling tool
Paintbrushes

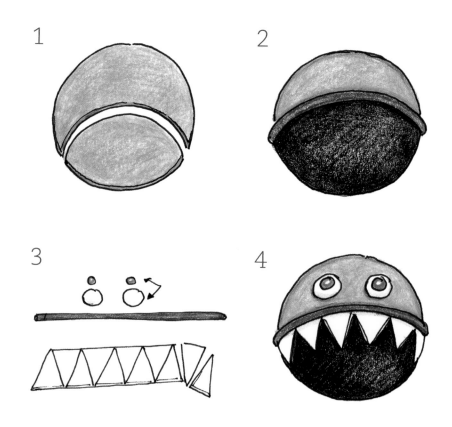

1. Use the circle cutter to cut the green icing and then cut again to create the face.
2. Apply the face to the top half of the cupcake and then add the red lips. 3. Cut the white icing to make the teeth and eyes, roll the red icing for the lips and the orange icing for the pupils. 4. Apply the teeth and the eyes.

Syrup the cupcakes
Follow the instructions on how to syrup cupcakes (page 37).

Ganache the cupcakes
Follow the instructions on how to ganache cupcakes (page 37).

Cover the cupcakes
Knead the black icing to a pliable dough and roll out to ⅛ inch thick. Using a circle cutter in the same size as the cupcakes, cut out 12 circles and stick them onto the cupcakes (page 43).

Make the head
Roll out the green icing to ⅛ inch thick and using a circle cutter cut a circle the same size as the cupcake. Use the same cutter and cut a half section out (step 1). Stick the remaining crescent moon shape onto the cupcake with a little water; align with the icing at the rim.

Make the lips
Roll out a strip of red icing (the width of the cupcake) and thin it out towards the ends. Stick the roll on the joining line between the black and the green icing. Trim at the sides (step 2).

Make the teeth
Roll out one-third of the white icing to ⅛ inch thick. Cut a strip of ¾ x 4 inches with a clean knife. Cut a zigzag for the teeth (step 3). Stick five to six teeth straight below the red icing.

Make the eyes
Roll pieces of the remaining white icing into pea-size balls and stick two on each monster's head. Using a frilling tool, make a hole in the center of each ball. Roll very small balls of the orange icing and stick those into the holes of the white icing with a little water (steps 3+4).

Ladybugs cupcakes

Material
12 cupcakes
7 tablespoons syrup
9 oz ganache
1 lb 2 oz black icing (cupcakes and dots)
1 lb 2 oz red icing (wings)
Mung bean noodles
1¾ oz white icing (eyes)
1¾ oz black icing (eyes)
Cornstarch

Equipment
Skewer
Pastry brush
Cranked palette knife
Large and small rolling pins
Pasta machine
Plastic sheets
Set of circle cutters
Flexi-scraper
Small kitchen knife or paring knife
Frilling tool
Plastic drinking straw
Paintbrushes

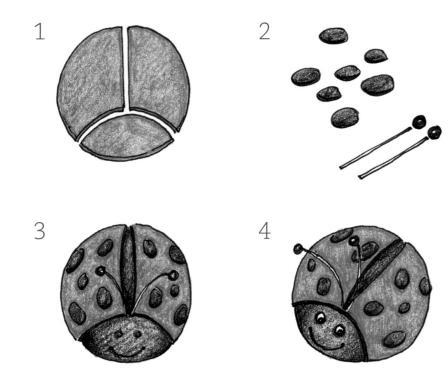

1. Use a round cutter to cut a disc of red icing for the wing cases. 2. Make the black spots and antennae. 3. Fix the spots to the wing cases with a dab of water and add the antennae. 4. Finish the eyes.

Syrup the cupcakes
Follow the instructions on how to syrup cupcakes (page 37).

Ganache the cupcakes
Follow the instructions on how to ganache cupcakes (page 37).

Cover the cupcakes
Knead 1 lb of the black icing to a pliable dough and roll out to ⅛ inch thick. Using a circle cutter in the same size as the cupcakes, cut out 12 circles and stick them onto the cupcakes (page 43).

Make the wing cases
Set aside a small quantity of red icing for the antennae, then roll out the red icing to ⅛ inch thick. Cut out discs, using a round cutter the same size as the cupcake. Use the round cutter to cut out one-quarter of the discs. Cut the remaining portion of the icing disc in half. Stick the two wing cases on the cupcake with a little water, moving them slightly apart (step 1).

Knead the remaining black icing and roll into baby pea-sized balls (step 2). Flatten the balls between your fingers and stick them on the wing cases (step 3).

Make the antennae
Roll two tiny balls of red or black icing and stick them on top of two short sticks of mung bean noodles. Poke the noodles into the cupcakes, just behind where the eyes will be (steps 2+3).

Make the face
With the frilling tool, indent two holes for the eyes. Use a drinking straw cut in half to mark the mouth. Roll out tiny balls of white icing and stick them into the indents. Using tiny amount of black icing, roll out even smaller balls and stick them on top of the white balls to finish the eyes (steps 3+4).

Pirate cupcakes

Material
12 cupcakes
7 tablespoons syrup
9 oz ganache
1 lb 2 oz skin-colored icing
   (mix red, orange, and brown)
   (cupcakes)
5½ oz red icing (bandana)
1¾ oz white icing (eye)
1¾ oz black icing (eye)
1½ oz black icing (eyepatch)
Gold dragees
Red and brown food coloring (scar)
Decorating alcohol
Cornstarch

Equipment
Skewer
Pastry brush
Cranked palette knife
Large and small rolling pins
Pasta machine
Plastic sheets
Set of circle cutters
Flexi-scraper
Small kitchen knife or paring knife
Frilling tool
Paintbrushes

Syrup the cupcakes
Follow the instructions on how to syrup cupcakes (page 37).

Ganache the cupcakes
Follow the instructions on how to ganache cupcakes (page 37).

Cover the cupcakes
Knead 1 lb of skin-colored icing to a pliable dough and roll out to ⅛ inch thick. Using a circle cutter in the same size as the cupcakes, cut out 12 circles and stick them on the cupcakes (page 43).

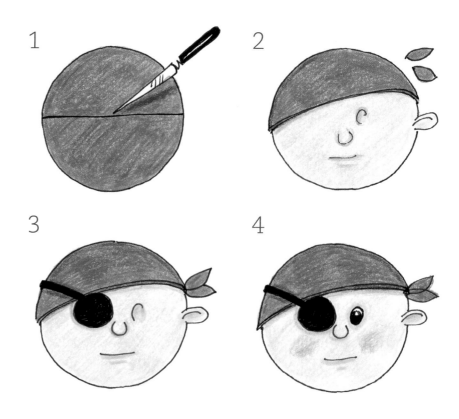

1. Cut a circle of the red icing in half. 2. Complete the bandana and mark the face. Add the ear. 3. Attach the eyepatch and strap. 4. Finish the eye with a dot of black icing.

Make the bandana
Roll out the red icing to ⅛ inch thick and cut out a disc with the same circle cutter. Cut the disc in half and stick onto the cupcake at an angle with a little water (steps 1+2). Cut out two small leaves and pinch them slightly together at one end. Stick them on the side of the bandana with a little water (step 2).

Make the face and scar
Roll a small ball of skin-colored icing for the nose and stick it onto the face with a little water. With the frilling tool, indent one hole for the eye. Roll out tiny balls of white icing and stick them into the indents. Using a tiny amount of black icing, roll out even smaller balls and stick them on top of the white balls.

Use a paring knife to make the pirate's mouth. Make a ball from skin-colored icing for the ear and stick it near the knot under the bandana. Press the frilling tool into the ball to make an ear shape (step 2). Stick one dragee into the ear as an earring and paint a scar (brown food coloring mixed with decorating alcohol) onto the face.

Make the eyepatch
Roll a bit of black icing to the size of a small pea, flatten it between your fingers and straighten it on one side. Stick it just below the bandana in line with the eye. Roll a very fine sausage out of the remaining black icing and stick on one side of the bandana across it to create the eyepatch strap (steps 3+4).

Naughty kids cupcakes

Material
12 cupcakes
7 tablespoons syrup
9 oz ganache
1 lb 2 oz skin-colored icing (mix red,
    orange, and brown) (cupcakes)
Red petal dust
Cornstarch
7 oz brown icing (hair)
7 oz black icing (hair)
7 oz orange icing (hair)
7 oz yellow icing (hair)
1¾ oz white icing (eyes)
1¾ oz black icing (eyes)

Equipment
Skewer
Pastry brush
Cranked palette knife
Large and small rolling pins
Pasta machine
Plastic sheets
Set of circle cutters
Flexi-scraper
Small kitchen knife or paring knife
Frilling tool
Paintbrushes

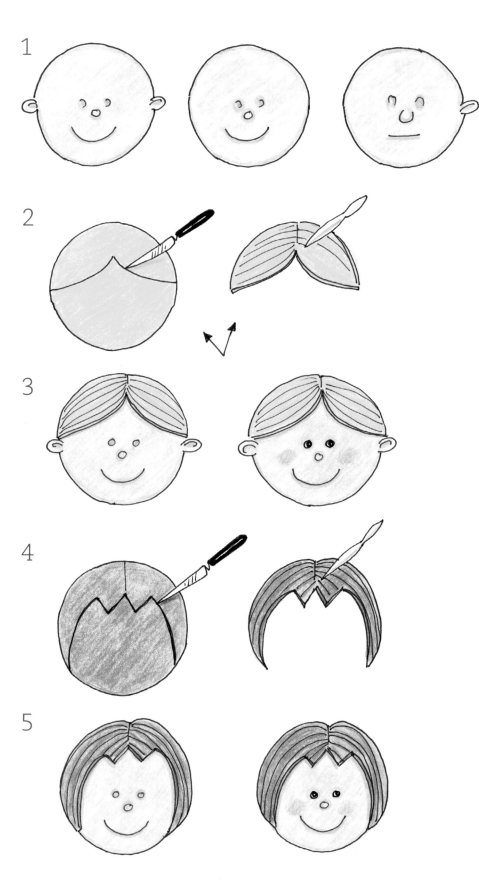

1. Use skin-colored icing for the face, add the nose and ears, and use the frilling tool to indent the eyes and freckles.

2. Cut the disc into the boy's hair shape and style with the frilling tool.

3. Apply the boy's hair with a dab of water and finish the eyes.

4. Cut the disc into the girl's hair shape and style with the frilling tool.

5. Apply the girl's hair and finish the eyes.

You can change the color of the hair and skin icing if you want them to resemble those you know.

Syrup the cupcakes
Follow the instructions on how to syrup cupcakes (page 37).

Ganache the cupcakes
Follow the instructions on how to ganache cupcakes (page 37).

Cover the cupcakes
Knead 1 lb of the skin-colored icing to a pliable dough and roll out to ⅛ inch thick. Using a circle cutter in the same size as the cupcakes, cut out 12 circles and stick them onto the cupcakes (page 43).

Make the face
Roll a small ball of the remaining skin-colored icing for the nose and stick it in the center of the face with a little water. With the frilling tool, mark two holes for the eyes and use the edge of a round cutter, or a knife, to indent the mouth.

Make two balls from skin-colored icing for the ears and stick them on either side of the boys' faces, level with the nose. Press the frilling tool into each ball to give them an ear shape (step 1). To give them a freckled look, mark small dots around the nose with the frilling tool.

Tip: Create the rosy cheeks by mixing red petal dust with cornstarch (to dilute) and dusting on with a dry paintbrush.

Make the hair
Roll brown, black, orange, and yellow icing to ⅛ inch thick. Using the same round cutter as for the skin, cut out a disc. Cut the disc into the boy's or girl's hair shape with a small knife. Use the frilling tool to add lines for a natural look (steps 2+4). Stick the hair onto the cupcake with a little water (steps 3+5).

Make the eyes
Roll out tiny balls of white icing and stick them into the eye indents. Roll out even smaller balls of black icing and stick them on top of the white balls to finish the eye. Cut a drinking straw in half lengthwise and poke it into the face to mark the eyebrows.

Crying babies cupcakes

Material
12 cupcakes
7 tablespoons syrup
9 oz ganache
1 lb 2 oz skin-colored icing
    (mix red, orange, and brown)
    (cupcakes)
7 oz black icing (mouth)
5½ oz red icing (tongue)
2¼ oz white icing (teeth)
Black food coloring
Decorating alcohol
2¼ oz yellow icing (quiffs)
Red petal dust
Cornstarch

Equipment
Skewer
Pastry brush
Cranked palette knife
Large and small rolling pins
Pasta machine
Plastic sheets
Set of circle cutters
Flexi-scraper
Small kitchen knife or paring knife
Frilling tool
Paintbrushes

1. Cover the cupcake and attach the ears. 2. Cut out the mouth and tongue. 3. Make the hair quiff and the teeth. 4. Use a fine paintbrush to add expression.

Syrup the cupcakes
Follow the instructions on how to syrup cupcakes (page 37).

Ganache the cupcakes
Follow the instructions on how to ganache cupcakes (page 37).

Cover the cupcakes
Knead 1 lb of skin-colored icing to a pliable dough and roll out to ⅛ inch thick. Using a circle cutter in the same size as the cupcakes, cut out 12 circles and stick them onto the cupcakes (page 43).

Make the ears
Make two balls of the remaining skin-colored icing and stick them on either side of the face. Press the frilling tool into each ball to create the ear shape (step 1).

Make the mouth
Roll out each of the black, red, and white icing to each ⅛ inch thick. Using a small circle cutter, cut a black circle for the mouth and stick it onto the face with a little water. Then, using an even smaller circle cutter, cut a red circle and cut the circle again for the tongue. Stick the tongue on the mouth (step 2).

With a sharp knife, cut the white icing into long thin strips and then into rectangles for the teeth (step 3), and stick two onto the mouth.

With a paintbrush paint a line on the tongue with black food coloring mixed with decorating alcohol (step 4).

Make the eyes
Use the paintbrush to paint two thin lines, like meeting chopsticks on the face, with black food coloring mixed with decorating alcohol (step 4).

Make the hair quiff
Roll out the yellow icing (or any color you wish) into a cone, then twist the cone between your fingers and stick it onto the head with a little water (steps 3+4).

Tip: For rosy cheeks, mix red petal dust with cornstarch, dust on the faces with a dry paintbrush.

Round cakes

The round cake is the simplest basic shape for beginner decorators — there are no tricky angles or corners to deal with. You'll be amazed to see what you can produce with the skills you have already mastered. (Of course, when you bring out your cake, don't tell anyone else how easy it was!)

For little boys who love their toy cars, or big boys who love their toys, this cake is a perennial winner. But what an easy place to start. This will introduce you to using a template.

Racing car cake

Materials
9-inch round cake
7 lengths no. 22 gauge wire
7 tablespoons syrup
3 lb 5 oz ganache
3 lb 5 oz blue icing (cake)
9 oz gray icing (border)
14 oz black icing (wheels
  and extras)
1 oz orange icing (hubcap)
2¼ oz red icing (cars)
2¼ oz green icing (cars)
2¼ oz yellow icing (cars)
2¼ oz orange icing (cars)
7 oz white icing (clouds and extras)
1 lb 9 oz white icing (board)
Glaze
Piping gel

Equipment
9-inch round board (set-up)
14-inch round board (display)
Ganaching tools (page 14)
Scissors
Hot glue or craft glue
Large and small rolling pins
Pasta machine
Plastic sheets
Small kitchen knife or paring knife
Flexi-scraper
Smoothers
Ruler
Pizza wheel
Balling tool (optional)
Set of circle cutters
No. 2 icing tip
Paintbrushes
Frilling tool
Wire cutters (secateurs)

Make the flags on wires
Use a photocopier to make 14 copies of the racing flag (page 189). Cut out and glue the flags to the top of the wires, using craft glue. Stick one copy on each side. Leave on a flat surface to dry (step 5, page 94).

Prepare the cake
Follow the instructions on how to prepare and ganache a round cake (page 38). Allow to set.

Cover the cake
Knead the blue icing to a pliable dough. Using a large rolling pin, roll out the icing to about ⅛ inch thick. Follow the instructions on how to cover a round cake (page 44).

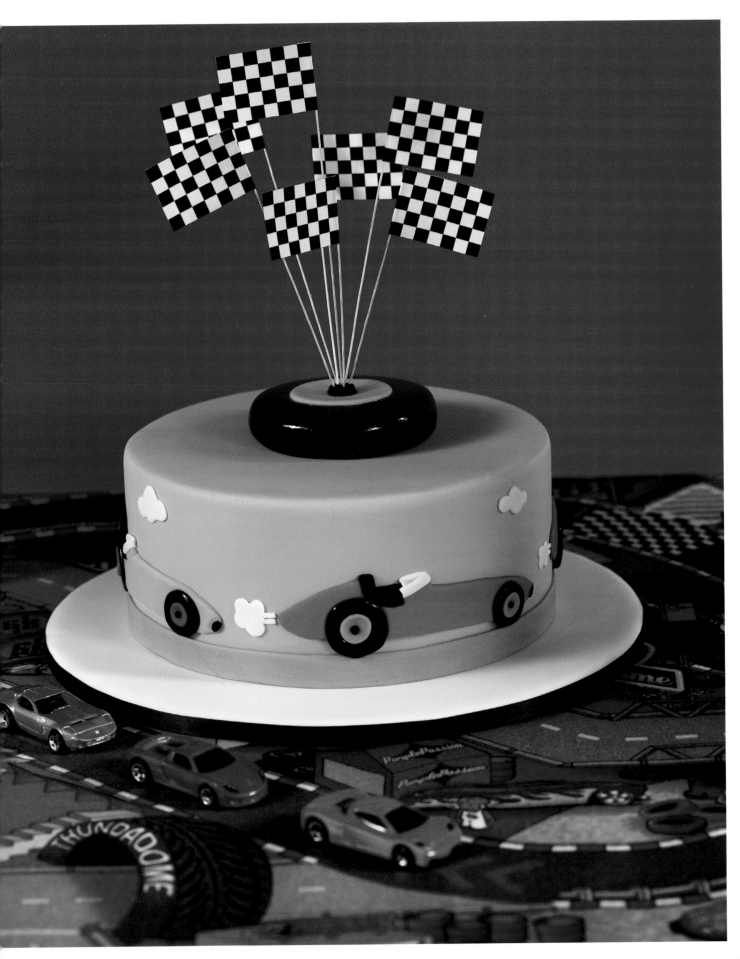

1. Make the road border.

2. Make the big wheel.

3. Assemble the wheel.

4. Cut out the cars and wheels.

5. Cut out the clouds and glue decorations on the cake.

6. Assemble the cake.

You can use the clouds to camouflage any rips or cracks in the icing.

Make the road border

Roll out the gray icing to ⅛ inch thick. Use a ruler and pizza wheel to cut a strip 16 inches long and 1 inch wide. Cover with plastic.

Lightly brush a line of water around the bottom of the cake to stick the strip on. Roll the strip onto a small rolling pin and unroll it around the cake. Overlap the icing at the join and cut it with a sharp knife so that it meets perfectly. This is now the back of the cake (step 1).

Make the big wheel

Roll out 1¾ oz of the black icing to ¾ inch thick. Use a 4-inch circle cutter to cut out the wheel. Mold and round the edges of the wheel with your fingers. Use a balling tool to indent the center of the wheel (step 2).

Roll out the orange icing to ⅛ inch thick, and use a large circle cutter to cut out the hubcap. Roll out a small amount of black icing and use an icing tip to cut the center of the hubcap. Mold into a dome.

Assemble the wheel

Place the hubcap and the center on the wheel and adjust the indent to fit. Fix with water and allow to dry.

Make the cars and clouds

Enlarge the car template (page 189), trace on waxed paper and cut it out. Roll out the four car colors to ⅛ inch thick, and cut out the cars (step 4). Use an icing tip to cut out eight mini hubcaps, two from each color. Cover the icing with plastic.

Roll out the black icing to ¼ inch thick, and use two small circle cutters (one slightly smaller than the other) to cut out eight tyres. Round the tyres slightly with your finger. Assemble the wheels, the smaller ones being the front wheels, using a dab of water. Add a small ball of flattened black icing in the center of the hubcaps (step 4).

Make the template for the clouds and exhaust smoke. Roll out the white icing to ⅛ inch thick and cut them out. Stick the clouds on with a dab of water (step 5).

Assemble the cars

Stick the cars on with water and polish with the flexi-scraper. Use your car template to create car trims from the white and black icings. A simple trim is a small, flattened roll of icing. Stick them on the cake with a little water. Do not polish with the flexi-scraper. Stick the car wheels on with water.

Attach the wheel

Stick the big wheel on the top of the cake with royal icing. Let dry.

Cover the display board

Knead the white icing to a pliable dough and roll out to ⅛ inch thick. Follow the instructions on how to cover a board (page 48).

Glaze (optional)

Follow the instructions on how to glaze (page 54). Glaze the wheels.

Place the flags

Trim the wires to create height variation and poke the flags into the center of the big wheel (step 6).

The decorations here are very crisp, clean, and effective — but also incredibly achievable for the beginner. The basic technique for cutting out the skull and crossbones can easily be applied to just about any design of your choice.

Pirate cake

Materials
9-inch round cake
7 tablespoons syrup
3 lb 5 oz ganache
2 lb 10 oz blue icing
1 lb 5 oz white icing (board)
7 oz white icing (skull and
    crossbones)
1¾ oz red icing (bandana)
3½ oz gray icing (cutlasses)
¾ oz black icing (handles)
1¾ oz yellow icing (stars)
7 oz red icing (seam)
Silver dragees
Decorating alcohol
Royal icing
Edible silver or gold dust
Cornstarch

Equipment
9-inch round board (set-up)
14-inch round board (display)
Ganaching tools (page 14)
Large and small rolling pins
Pasta machine
Plastic sheets
Cranked palette knife
Small kitchen knife or paring knife
Flexi-scraper
Smoothers
Frilling tool
Paintbrush
Star cutters (various sizes)

Prepare the cake
Follow the instructions on how to prepare and ganache a round cake (page 38).

Cover the cake
Knead the blue icing to a pliable dough. Roll out to ⅛ inch and follow the instructions on how to cover a round cake (page 44).

Cover the display board
Knead the white icing to a pliable consistency. Follow the instructions on how to cover a board (page 48).

Decorate the side with dragees
Straight after covering the cake and while the icing is still soft, use the frilling tool to make small indents in the side of the cake in a random pattern. Press one cachou into each indent.

1. Apply the syrup and ganache.

2. Cover and smooth the cake.

3. Cover the board.

4. Cut out the skull and crossbones using the template.

5. Cut out the cutlasses and stars for the side decorations.

6. Apply the decorations.

For a three-dimensional effect, place tissue paper underneath the flaps, so that they are slightly raised and remove when the icing has dried.

Use the flexi-scraper to smooth the side of the cake, so that the dragees are even with the icing.

Tip: Avoid marking the icing with your fingerprints by using a frilling tool. If the dragees are not sticking to the icing, attach them with a little royal icing.

Create the template cut-outs
For the skull and crossbones, enlarge the template (page 187) on a photocopier, trace it on waxed paper and cut it out. Roll out the 7 oz of white icing in a pasta machine, or with a rolling pin, to about ⅛ inch thick. Lightly dust a board with cornstarch and place your rolled icing on it. Let the icing dry slightly.

Lay the paper template on top of the icing and trace the outline of the skull, then lift off the paper. Using a paring knife, cut the skull and crossbones shape out of the icing. Stick them onto the cake with a dab of water.

For the bandana, follow the instructions on how to trace and cut out a shape, as you did with the skull and crossbones.

Stick the bandana above the skull with a little water. For the little bandana knot flaps, use the remaining red icing to cut out a 2½ x 1½ inch strip. Cut the long side on a 45° angle to make two triangles (step 4).

Pinch the short side of the triangles into a few pleats and trim the edges. Stick both pleated triangles on the right side of the bandana with a little water (step 6).

Decorate the side
For the cutlasses, knead the gray icing to a pliable consistency, and then roll it out to ⅛ inch thick.

Follow the instructions on how to trace and cut out a shape, as you did with the skull and crossbones. Paint the cutlasses with silver dust (page 61), and stick them on the cake, while they are still soft, with a little water.

For the handles, roll a small sausage of black icing and mold it into two handles. Stick the handles on the cake at the end of the blade with a little water (step 6).

For the stars, knead the yellow icing to a pliable consistency, then roll out to ⅛ inch thick. Using different-sized cutters, cut out stars and stick them on the side of the cake with a little water, placing them at random.

Base seam
Knead the 7 oz of red icing to a pliable consistency. Using an icing smoother, roll the icing into a roll (page 62). Brush a line of water on the bottom around the cake and carefully roll the cord around it, starting at the back. Roll a small ball out of the remaining red icing to cover the join.

The present box is a wonderfully simple idea that looks great in any color, or combination of colors. This cake introduces you to a number of techniques, such as making a bow and a lid and creating stripes.

Present box cake

Materials
9-inch round cake
7 tablespoons syrup
3 lb 5 oz ganache
3 lb 5 oz white icing (cake)
1 lb 5 oz white icing (board)
1 lb 5 oz blue icing (lid and strips)
1 lb 2 oz white icing (strips
   and ribbon)
7 oz white icing (seam)
9 oz white icing (bow)
¾ oz white icing (tag) (optional)
1¾ oz blue royal icing (tag)
   (optional)
Tissue paper

Equipment
9-inch round board (set-up)
14-inch round board (display)
Ganaching tools (page 14)
Large and small rolling pins
Pasta machine
Plastic sheets
Cranked palette knife
Small kitchen knife or paring knife
Flexi-scraper
Smoothers
Pizza wheel
Ruler
Paintbrush
Icing bag
No. 2 icing tip

Prepare the cake
Follow the instructions on how to prepare and ganache a round cake (page 38).

Cover the cake
Knead the white icing for the cake to a pliable dough and roll out to ⅛ inch thick, using a large rolling pin. Follow the instructions on how to cover a round cake (page 44).

Cover the display board
Knead the white icing for the board to a pliable dough and roll out to ⅛ inch thick. Follow the instructions on how to cover a board, using either method (page 48).

1. Cover the cake and board. Add strips of icing to the side of the cake.

2. Use a ruler to mark the edge of the lid all around the cake.

3. Place measured icing strips across the cake.

4. Make a thin icing roll to cover the base.

5. Prepare the bow and tag. Use tissue paper to keep the bow in shape until dry.

6. Attach the bow and tag.

To create soft, elegant bow loops, fill them with cotton wool and remove when the icing has dried.

Make the ribbon

Knead 9 oz of the white icing to a pliable dough and roll out to a 6¼ x 8 inch rectangle. Cut the rectangle into four long 1½-inch wide strips. Trim one end of each ribbon into a V-shape to help join the ribbons at the top. Stick onto the cake with water and trim excess ends with a knife (step 3).

Make the base seam

Knead the white icing for the seam into a pliable dough and roll it into a thin roll that is long enough to fit around the cake (page 62). Lay the icing roll around the base of the cake and trim at the joining line (step 4). Roll a little ball out of the remaining white icing and stick it onto the joining line with a little water.

Make the bow

Knead the white icing for the bow into a pliable dough. Follow the instructions on how to make a bow (page 58).

Make the tag (optional)

Make your own template to cut a rectangle out of the white icing, and cut off two triangles on both sides to achieve a pointy side, using a small knife. Smooth the edges with your finger. Using the end of your icing tube, make a hole in the end of the tag (step 5). Bend the tag a little for a more realistic look. Allow the tag to dry and harden, then stick it on your cake. Using a no. 2 icing tip, pipe out a name or word on the tag (page 56).

Place the bow and the tag

Place the bow on top of the cake on the joining line on top of the ribbon. Knead ¾ oz of the left-over blue icing and then roll it thinly into a sausage. Thread the thin roll through the hole in the tag and attach it to the bow with a little water.

Make the strips

Measure the circumference of the cake, and divide it into equal parts. It needs to be an even number; for instance, if your cake is 11 inches in circumference, each of the strips should be ½ inch wide. Roll out 9 oz of the blue and 9 oz of the 1 lb 2 oz white icing to ⅛ inch thick.

Use a pizza wheel, or a sharp small knife, to cut ten 1¼-inch wide strips in blue and ten matching strips in white, to a length that is approximately the height of the cake. Cover the strips with plastic to prevent the icing drying out.

Using a paintbrush dampened with water (or syrup), brush a small line on the cake to make the icing sticky (page 54).

Stick the first strip on the cake, starting from the bottom edge and moving up to the top. Trim the top end of the strip with a knife (step 1). Repeat, alternating the color, until all the strips are placed on the cake.

Make the lid

Let the cake sit for a couple of hours to allow the icing to dry before you make the lid.

Brush the top of the cake with a little water (or syrup) and run the brush around the top 1 inch of the side of the cake.

Knead 10½ oz of the blue icing to a pliable dough. Roll the icing to at least 8 inches larger than the diameter of the cake. Roll the icing over your rolling pin, lift it up and roll it over the cake. Smooth the top and sides with a flexi-scraper. Use a ruler to mark the edge of the lid all around the side of the cake (step 2).

Make sure the ruler mark is lower than the water line, otherwise the icing will be sloppy below the line of the lid. Trim the lid with a sharp clean knife.

I can think of a lot of adults who would love this cake — and with the color and name changed it could also be made for a king or queen. The princess cake introduces you to frilling, cut-outs, decorating using an icing bag, and painting in gold.

Princess cake

Materials
9-inch round cake
7 tablespoons syrup
3 lb 5 oz ganache
2 lb 10 oz pink icing (cake)
2 lb 7 oz white icing (board, collar, crown, and letters)
Gold dragees
9 oz hot pink icing (seam)
Decorating alcohol
3½ oz white royal icing
Edible gold dust

Equipment
9-inch round board (set-up)
14-inch round board (display)
7-inch round board (template)
Ganaching tools (page 14)
Large and small rolling pins
Pasta machine
Plastic sheets
Cranked palette knife
Flexi-scraper
Plastic scraper
Smoothers
Frilling tool
Pizza wheel
Ruler
Paintbrush
Scissors
Icing bag
No. 1 and no. 2 icing tips
Alphabet cutters

Prepare the cake
Follow the instructions on how to prepare and ganache a round cake (page 38).

Cover the cake
Knead the pink icing to a pliable dough and roll out to ⅛ inch thick. Follow the instructions on how to cover a round cake (page 44).

Cover the display board
Knead 1 lb 9 oz of the white icing to a pliable dough. Follow the instructions on how to cover a round board, using either method (page 48).

Decorate the side with dragees
Straight after covering the cake and while the icing is still soft, make small indents in the side of the cake

1. Cover the prepared and ganached cake and board.

2. Attach the frilled collar.

3. Roll little balls of icing and place them around the base of the cake.

4. Pipe the design on the crown and paint.

5. Paint the rolled icing and cut out the letters.

6. Place the crown and lettering on the cake.

in a random pattern, using a frilling tool. Press the dragees carefully into the indents (step 1). Use the flexi-scraper to smooth the side of the cake so the dragees sit flush with the icing.

Note: If the icing is not soft and the dragees don't stay on it, you can stick them on with a little royal icing.

Make the frilled collar
Knead 7 oz of the white icing into a pliable dough and roll out to ⅛ inch thick.

Using a pizza wheel, cut out two strips of about 1¼ inches wide and about 12 inches long. Cover the icing strips with a plastic sheet to prevent them from drying out.

Place one of the strips on a clean work surface lightly dusted with cornstarch and, using a frilling tool or a stick, roll along the side of the strip. Roll the tool back and forth to thin out the icing to achieve a frilly look (page 61).

Brush a fine line of water around the top edge of the cake. Place the template board on the cake as a guide for the frilled collar (step 2). Stick the first frilled strip on the water line while pleating the icing with your fingers to get a fabric effect (step 2). Repeat with the second strip and join the frilly strips by overlapping the ends.

Make the balls for the base seam
Knead the hot pink icing to a pliable dough. Roll out a strip to about the thickness of your little finger and to about 12 inches long. Cut the roll into about 50 slices in two different sizes. Keep the icing covered with plastic to prevent it from drying out.

Run a line of water around the bottom edge of the cake. Roll the icing pieces into balls varying in size and place them next to each other on the side of the cake in a random pattern (step 3).

The charm of this cake lies in the delicacy of the frill and the beautifully decorated crown. Instead of using alphabet cutters you could pipe a name or word on the cake.

Pipe along the frilled collar
Fill an icing bag with white royal icing, using a no. 2 tip. Pipe little dots around the inner edge of the frilled collar on top of the cake to cover the joining line (step 3). Follow the instructions on how to pipe (page 56).

Make the crown
Enlarge the crown template (page 186), trace on waxed paper and cut it out.

Knead 3½ oz of the white icing to a pliable dough and roll out to ¼ inch thick. Place the template on the icing and cut around it. Take the template off and smooth the edges with your finger.

Fill an icing bag with white royal icing, using a no. 2 tip. Pipe little dots on the crown to create an attractive pattern. Let the royal icing dry, then paint the crown with gold dust mixed with decorating alcohol. While the color is still wet, stick golden dragees on it for decoration (step 4).

Make the letters
Knead 3½ oz of the white icing to a pliable dough. Roll out to ¼ inch thick, using a pasta machine or a rolling pin. Let the icing dry, then paint it with gold dust mixed with decorating alcohol. Let it dry, then cut out the letters you need for the word or name you want to put on your cake (step 5).

Smooth the edges of the letters with your fingertip, and then stick the letters on the cake with a little water.

Tip: If you don't have alphabet cutters create your own letters by tracing them on a piece of paper or cardboard and then cut them out. Use the same process as for making the crown.

Place the crown and letters
Once the crown and letters are dry, carefully lift them up and stick them onto the cake using a little water (step 6).

If you have any apprehensions at all about your skills, the lollipop cake makes a fantastic place to start. The techniques and decorations consist of nothing more complicated than coloring icing and creating rolls and a bow, yet the results are stunning.

Lollipop cake

Materials
9-inch round cake
7 tablespoons syrup
3 lb 5 oz ganache
2¼ lb pink icing (cake)
2¾ lb white icing (board)
7 oz yellow icing (coil)
7 oz pink icing (coil)
1¾ oz green icing (coil)
1¾ oz blue icing (coil)
10½ oz caramel icing (stick)
14 oz red icing (bow)

Equipment
Two 9-inch round boards (set-up)
18 x 12 inch rectangular cake board
  (display)
Ganaching tools (page 14)
Large and small rolling pins
Pasta machine
Plastic sheets
Cranked palette knife
Small kitchen knife or paring knife
Flexi-scraper
Plastic scraper
Smoothers
Paintbrush

Prepare the cake
Follow the instructions on how to prepare and ganache a round cake (page 38).

Cover the cake
Knead the pink icing to a pliable dough and roll out to ⅛ inch thick. Follow the instructions on how to cover a round cake (page 44).

Cover the display board
Knead the white icing to a pliable dough and roll out to ⅛ inch thick, using a large rolling pin. Follow the instructions on how to cover a board (page 48).

1. Cover the cake and position at one end of the board, leaving the other end free for the stick.

2. Coil the four colors together on a round board and roll flat.

3. Slide the coil onto the cake.

4. Position the stick.

5. Make the bow and attach it on the stick.

6. Add the finishing touches.

The appeal of this cake lies in the fact that the stripes don't have to be absolutely perfect.

Lollipop colors

Knead the four colored lollipop icings individually to a pliable dough, using a little cornstarch on the work surface, if needed. Use a rolling pin to roll out each color to a strip about the thickness of your index finger. Use an acrylic smoother to create an even roll (page 62), and then cover with plastic. Roll all the colors to the same length, including the smaller quantities (these rolls will be thinner). Start rolling all four cords into a coil on a 9-inch round board. Roll the huge coil flat until it fills the whole board (step 2). Slide the coil onto the cake (step 3). Lift the coil carefully and brush the cake with water so the coil sticks.

Lollipop stick

Knead the caramel icing to a pliable dough and roll it out to about 8 inches long. Stick it onto the board at the bottom of the lollipop with a little water (step 4).

Make the bow

Knead the red icing to a pliable dough. Follow the instructions on how to make a bow (page 58).

Place the bow

Stick one loop of the bow on the board with a little water, right next to the lollipop stick, about halfway down. Repeat with the second bow loop, sticking it on the other side of the lollipop stick.

Pleat the square piece of icing into a few folds, making sure the raw edge is positioned on the inside (step 5). Stick the pleated icing onto the lollipop stick between the two bow loops, so that it looks like a bow tied around the stick (steps 5+6).

Square cakes

So now you've progressed from round cakes to squares and rectangles. The tricky bit of decorating cakes with angles is knowing what to do with all that icing when you reach the corners.

This cake can be made even easier by keeping the sails a plain color rather than coloring them with spots and stripes. This cake shows the effectiveness of cut-outs and simple modelling.

Boat cake

Materials
8-inch square cake
9 oz white icing (sails)
9 oz blue icing (sails)
4 wooden skewers
Piping gel
½ inch satin ribbon (flags)
10½ oz white icing (spinnakers)
3½ oz blue icing (spots)
3½ oz yellow icing (spots)
3½ oz white icing (boats)
8-inch square cake
7 tablespoons syrup
3 lb 5 oz ganache
3 lb 5 oz light blue icing (cake)
2¼ lb blue icing (board and wave)
7 oz red icing (buoy)
7 oz white icing (buoy and rope)

Equipment
14-inch square board (display)
8-inch square board (set-up)
Ganaching tools (page 14)
Scissors
Large and small rolling pins
Pasta machine
Plastic sheets
Small kitchen knife or paring knife
Flexi-scraper
Smoothers
Pizza wheel
Ruler
Paintbrushes
Hot glue (optional)
Glue gun (optional)
Set of circle cutters or icing tips

Make the sails
Enlarge the template (page 188) on a photocopier. Trace on waxed paper and cut it out. Roll out the white and blue icing into large squares ¼ inch thick. Cut the icing into ½ inch wide strips, then glue the alternate colors together with a paintbrush and a thin line of water (step 1).

Roll over the icing with a rolling pin so that the strips come together. Place your template on top to make sure you can cut four sails out of the strips (step 1, page 116). Leave the icing until it has dried a little but is still soft.

Use the template to cut out the sail. Stick the sail to a skewer with piping gel, leaving room for the flag at the top. Leave to dry.

1. Cut out the sails and fix them to the skewers. Add the flags.

2. Make the spinnakers.

3. Make the boats, rope, and buoy.

4. Cover the cake.

5. Make the wave.

6. Assemble the cake.

If you want to personalize the cake you can pipe a name onto the boats before you stick them onto the cake.

Trim the skewer to size. Cut flags from the satin ribbon and glue to the top of the skewer using a hot glue gun. Repeat to make four sails.

Make the spinnakers
Roll out the white icing to ⅛ inch thick and large enough to cut out four spinnakers. Roll out the blue and yellow icings to ⅛ inch thick. Use 2 to 3 small circle cutters, or icing tips, to cut out circles in the white icing and replace them with the same size circles from the yellow and blue icings (step 2).

Roll over the decorated icing very lightly with a rolling pin and cut out the spinnaker shapes using the template. Set aside to harden.

Make the boats
Roll out the white icing to ¼ inch thick and large enough to cut out four boats. Place the template on the icing and cut around the outlines (step 3). Set aside and allow to harden.

Prepare the cake
Follow the instructions on how to prepare and ganache a square cake (page 37).

Cover the cake
Knead the light blue icing to a pliable dough and roll out to ⅛ inch thick. Follow the instructions on how to cover a square cake (page 46).

Make the wave border
Roll out 7 oz of the blue icing to ⅛ inch thick. Use a ruler and a pizza wheel to cut a 1½-inch wide rectangular strip long enough to wrap around the cake. Working quickly so the icing does not dry, use a ½-inch circle cutter to cut out semicircles from the top border to create the wave effect. Lightly brush around the bottom of the cake with water to stick the border on (step 5). Roll the wave border onto a small rolling pin and unroll around the sides of the cake, smoothing and pressing as you go.

Make the rope and buoy
Follow the instructions on how to make an icing roll (page 62). Roll out 5½ oz of the white icing into two 12-inch long rolls. Twist the rolls to make the rope. Make a thick red roll. Join the ends and stick them together with a little water. Roll out the remaining white icing to ⅛ inch thick, then cut four small white strips to decorate the red ring. Wrap the squares around the ring, making sure to cover the join (step 3).

Cover the display board
Knead the remaining blue icing to a pliable dough. Roll out to ⅛ inch thick. Follow the instructions on how to cover a board (page 48).

Assemble the cake
Arrange the buoy and rope on the cake before the rope hardens. Stick the boats on with a little water, leaving enough room for the sails. Stick the trimmed skewers on the cake, then stick on the spinnakers.

I love this cake design because it's so versatile. Once you've mastered the blueprint you can create suitcases, beauty cases and laptop bags. You could make luggage labels or address tags. If you're a beginner, simplify the design by making the handle from solid icing only and using a single color for the tie.

Briefcase cake

Materials
8-inch square cake
12-inch aquarium tube
2 wooden skewers or dowels
1 lb dark brown icing (handle and attachements)
Piping gel
7 oz dark brown icing (decoration)
7 tablespoons syrup
3 lb 5 oz ganache
3 lb 5 oz brown icing (cake)
2¼ lb white icing (board)
10½ oz caramel icing (gold detail)
Edible gold dust
Decorating alcohol
¾ lb red icing (tie)
¾ lb white icing (tie)
¾ lb blue icing (tie)
1¾ oz royal icing
Cornstarch

Equipment
12 x 8 inch board (set-up)
16-inch square board (display)
Ganaching tools (page 14)
Scissors
Large and small rolling pins
Pasta machine
Plastic sheets
Small kitchen knife or paring knife
Flexi-scraper
Paintbrushes
2 smoothers
Ruler
Stitching tool
Set of circle cutters
No. 2 icing tip
Frilling tool

Make the handle
This method will give the handle a very realistic look. A less fiddly way is to make it from solid icing. Follow the same instructions but replace the tubes with a sausage of 3½ oz of dark brown icing and allow extra time for drying.

Enlarge the template (page 187) on a photocopier, trace on waxed paper and cut it out. Place a skewer in each end of the tubing, making sure it is long enough to insert into the cake. If the skewers are loose, insert a few toothpicks to tighten. Brush the tube with piping gel.

To cover the tube, roll out 5½ oz of the dark brown icing to ⅛ inch thick and cut into a rectangle large enough to fold over the handle, allowing for some overhang of about ½ inch. Trim off the excess icing and smooth down the seam with your fingers.

1. Shape and ganache the cake.

2. Cover the cake and use a ruler to mark the edge of the lid.

3. Use the stitching tool to decorate the edges of the lid and the seam on the handle.

4. Make the catches and the four corner caps.

5. Roll out the colored icings and make the tie.

6. Assemble the cake.

Now roll out 7 oz of the dark brown icing to ⅛ inch thick. Use your template to cut out two pieces of dark brown icing. Cover with plastic to prevent drying out. Brush the covered handle with water and stick the two pieces on top. Smooth the joining line with your fingers. With a stitching tool or a toothpick, stitch marks along the sides of the handle.

Make the handle attachments

Roll out the remaining dark brown icing to make a small cylinder about 1½ inches long and ¾ inch in diameter. Cut the cylinder in half crosswise and stick onto the skewers at the bottom of the handle (step 3).

Prepare the cake

Follow the instructions on how to make and ganache a 12 x 8 inch rectangular cake (page 40). Place the cake on the set-up board.

Cover the cake

Knead the brown icing to a pliable dough and roll out to ⅛ inch thick. Follow the instructions on how to cover a square cake (page 46). Quickly move to the next step while the icing is still soft.

Cover the display board

Follow the instructions on how to cover a board (page 48). Place the cake onto the board.

Indent the lid

To create the lid, mark a line around the sides of the cake about one-third from the top using a ruler. Mark both sides of the line with the stitching tool (steps 2+3).

Make the catches and the corners

For the catches, roll out 7 oz of the caramel icing to ⅛ inch and cut the shapes. Stick them on the cake with a bit of water. Make four small

Paint the buckles and catches in gold to give them a realistic look.

balls and stick them underneath the corners as leg rests.

For the corners, roll out 7 oz of the dark brown icing to ⅛ inch and cut out two large circles of 3¼ inches in diameter with a circle cutter. Cut the circles in half and place one on each corner of the lid with a dab of water.

Cut out four rectangles to the diameter of the circles and about ¾ inch wide. Stick them on the bottom corners with a dab of water. Mark each corner cap with the stitching tool (step 4).

To create the base of the gold detail on each corner, cut out six circles from the caramel icing with a 2½-inch circle cutter, then cut two of these in half for the bottom corners. Place a full circle on the corners of the lid with a dab of water and do the same with the half circles for the bottom corners.

Create the screws on the smaller circles with a no. 2 icing tip.

Make the handle base

To create the gold detail at the bottom of the handle, roll out the caramel icing to about ⅛ inch thick and cut two squares about the size of postage stamps. Then make two thick discs slightly smaller than the squares. Use the handle as a guide to help you place the bases in the correct position. Stick them to the briefcase with a dab of water, placing the discs on top of the squares (step 3).

Paint the buckles and corner caps with gold powder mixed with decorating alcohol (page 61).

Push the handle into the lower side of the front of the cake and let it rest on the board.

Make and place the tie

Enlarge the tie template (page 187) on a photocopier, trace on waxed paper and cut it out. Roll out two strips of the red, white, and blue icing into large rectangles ¼ inch thick, using your tie template as a guide for the width required (step 5).

Use a pizza wheel, or sharp knife, to cut the three icings into thin strips and then glue the alternate colors together with a paintbrush and a thin line of water. Roll over the icing with a rolling pin so that the strips come together. Leave the icing until it has dried a little but is still soft. Place the template on top of the icing and cut out the tie, knot, and neckpiece (step 5).

Fold the neckpiece in half lengthwise, form a loop and place it on the briefcase. Pinch the top of the tie to create creases and stick it on the joining line under the tie loop on the briefcase. Wrap the tie knot around it to cover the joining lines. Secure the tie with a brush of water (step 6).

This cake design using wire decorations can easily be adapted to just about any occasion. For Valentine's Day, change the color and use hearts instead of stars. (We've even been asked to make this with flying pigs on the wires!)

Exploding star cake

Material
8-inch square cake
7 tablespoons syrup
3 lb 5 oz ganache
20 x 16-inch no. 22 gauge wire
2 x 1 oz green icing (stars)
2 x 1 oz yellow icing (stars)
2 x 1 oz red icing (stars)
2 x 1 oz light blue icing (stars)
3½ oz orange icing (numbers)
2 x 1 oz red icing (explosion rip)
3 lb 5 oz blue icing (cake)
1 lb 5 oz black icing (board)
5½ oz red icing (ribbon)
3½ oz orange icing (seam)
Silver dragees
Cornstarch

Equipment
8-inch square board (set-up)
14-inch square board (display)
Number cutters (or DIY template)
Ganaching tools (page 14)
Large and small rolling pins
Pasta machine
Plastic sheets
Small kitchen knife or paring knife
Flexi-scraper
Smoothers
Star cutters
Paintbrushes
Frilling tool
Wire cutters (secateurs)
Set of circle cutters
Ruler
Pizza wheel

Prepare the cake
Follow the instructions on how to prepare and ganache a square cake (page 39).

Make the stars and numbers
To make the stars, roll out one portion of the star colors to ⅛ inch thick. Use star cutters to cut out 15 to 20 different-sized stars. Cover with plastic. Stick the end of the wires into water and push into the stars. Set aside to dry on a flat surface.

For the numbers, roll out the orange icing to ¼ inch thick. Cut out the numbers. Stick two more wires into water and push into each number. Let dry. Trim the wires to differentiate them in height from the stars (step 1, page 124).

1

2

1. Make the stars and numbers.

2. Create the explosion rip.

3. Cover the cake and cut the rip.

4. Fold back the triangles and add the ribbon.

5. Decorate the sides with stars and some dragees.

6. Place stars and numbers.

3

4

5

6

Create the explosion rip

Read the instructions on how to cover a square cake (page 46) before you start.

Brush your cake with syrup. Roll out each explosion rip icing piece to ⅛ inch thick. Use a 3¼-inch circle cutter to cut out two circles. Place the circles on top of each other in the center of the cake and brush only the top of the top circle with syrup (step 2).

Cover the cake

Knead the blue icing to a pliable dough. Roll out to ⅛ inch thick and follow the instructions on how to cover a square cake. With a small knife, cut four lines through the blue icing and into the circle so you end up with eight triangles (take care to cut only through the top circle and not through to the cake). Pull the triangles outwards, so that they curl back like a flower, exposing the color underneath (steps 3+4).

Make the ribbon

Roll the red icing in the pasta machine, or by hand, to ⅛ inch thick. Use a ruler and pizza wheel to cut four strips about 8 inches long and 1 inch wide.

Cut a V into one end of each strip. Cover with a plastic sheet to prevent it drying out (step 4).

Brush a line of water on all four sides of the cake and stick a strip onto it. Starting from the top, curl the strips back just under the explosion rip to create the effect of a present that has just been opened.

Take the strips along the side of the cake and trim flush on the base with a sharp knife.

Cover the display board

Roll out the black icing to ⅛ inch thick. Follow the instructions on how to cover a board (page 48).

This cake is great for anniversaries and birthday parties. With a set of number cutters you are able to create any number you want.

Make the decorative stars

Roll out the remaining portions of the star colors to ⅛ inch thick. Cut out the stars and cover with plastic to prevent them drying out. Stick half of the stars in a random pattern on the cake with water.

With a frilling tool, poke indentations in the sides of the cake and place dragees. Polish with the flexi-scraper.

Tip: The stars can be used to cover any cracks in the icing.

Cover the base seams

Knead the orange icing to a pliable consistency and then, using an acrylic smoother, roll it into a roll (page 62). Brush a line of water along the bottom of the cake and carefully roll the cord around it, starting at the back. Cover the joining line with a ball of icing.

Place the stars and numbers

Wind the wire of the stars around a pencil, then pull out the pencil. Be careful not to damage the stars. Arrange the stars and numbers on the cake just as you would a bunch of flowers.

Fill the explosion rip with the silver dragees.

Tip: Create as much height variation as possible by trimming the wires.

This cake is quite fiddly — rather than cutters and templates, you'll need your modelling skills for creating the turntable arm and knobs. When you start creating realistic cakes like this, if you don't have a real record player to look at it's always helpful to have a photo to work from.

Record player cake

Materials
10-inch square cake (see Note)
7 tablespoons syrup
3 lb 5 oz ganache
3 lb 5 oz orange icing (cake)
1 lb 5 oz gray icing (turntable and shifter)
1¾ oz blue icing (knobs)
¼ inch piece wooden dowel
Edible silver dust
Decorating alcohol
1 lb 9 oz white icing (board)
7-inch long wooden dowel with ¼ inch diameter (arm)
Piping gel
No. 20 gauge wire
3½ oz black icing (record)
1¾ oz red icing (record label)
7 oz royal icing
Cornstarch

Equipment
14-inch square board (display)
10-inch square board (set-up)
8-inch round board (turntable template)
7-inch round board (record template)
Waxed cardboard 2½ x ¾ inch rectangle (DIY template)
Ganaching tools (page 14)
Large and small rolling pins
Pasta machine
Plastic sheets
Small kitchen knife or paring knife
Flexi-scraper
Smoother
Frilling tool
No. 3 icing tip
Set of oval cutters
Set of circle cutters
Paintbrushes
Wire cutters (secateurs)
Pizza wheel

Shape and ganache the cake
This is a great trick to save you sculpting time. Use one of the 8-inch square cake recipes and quantities, but bake your cake in a 10-inch cake pan. The cake will bake much lower, creating the size you want for the turntable shape which is 10 x 10 inch square and about 1½ inch high. Slice the cake in half horizontally, then sandwich together with ganache. Follow the instructions on how to ganache a square cake (page 39).

Note: The cake will need about 10 to 15 minutes less time to bake in the bigger cake pan.

Cover the cake
Knead the orange icing to a pliable dough. Roll out to ⅛ inch thick and follow the instructions on how to cover a square cake (page 46).

127

Using a pastry brush for glazing the record will give it a nice shiny look as well as the typical record grooves.

Make the pitch shifter

While the icing is still soft, stamp the control for the pitch shifter at the far bottom right of the cake using the template (page 189). Use the back of a knife to make the impression down the center (step 3).

Make the turntable

Roll out 10½ oz of the gray icing to ½ inch thick. Use the round 8-inch cake board as a template to cut out the turntable. Place the icing circle on the board and cut around it, holding your knife at an angle to create a bevelled edge. Position the turntable towards the left side of the cake and stick it on with a little water. Use the frilling tool to create a pattern around the sides (step 2, page 131).

Glaze (optional)

Follow the instructions on how to glaze (page 54). Glaze the icing while it is still soft, using a pastry brush.

Make the knobs and player controls

Roll out 1¾ oz of each of the blue and gray icing to ⅛ inch thick. Create the knobs and controls using the icing tip and oval cutters (step 3). Cut out the smaller buttons with an icing tip. Cut out a larger blue circle and place a thin roll of icing around it. For the large cylindrical knob in the front, insert a wooden dowel and cover it with gray icing. Model it into shape using your fingers and with a flat knife create the flat sides. Stick the knobs and controls onto the cake with a little water (step 4).

Mix the edible silver dust with decorating alcohol and paint the knobs and controls. If you wish, you can paint the play buttons in black. Allow the silver to dry and mix black food coloring and decorating alcohol and paint over the top, being careful not to smudge.

Cover the display board

Knead the white icing to a pliable dough. Follow the instructions on how to cover a board, using either method (page 48).

Using a very fine paintbrush, paint details such as for the play button and the volume control shifter.

Make the arm, arm holder, arm head and needle

For the arm, use a 7-inch long wooden dowel and brush it with piping gel. Roll out 3½ oz of the gray icing to ⅛ inch thick. Cut a 7 x ½ inch strip and wrap the icing around the gelled dowel. Trim the ends and allow to dry.

Roll out two thin 1¼ x ½ inch strips of icing and wrap them around the arm using your fingers, smoothing and sticking them on with piping gel as you go. Trim, making sure the seam is underneath.

For the head and needle, use a bit of the left-over gray icing, the size of a walnut, and with your fingers and icing smoothers mold a needle head shape. Skewer it to the end of the record arm with piping gel and disguise the seam with a thin piece of icing or thin icing roll attached with piping gel. Trim the wire to a short piece and position it in the end of the record head. Allow to dry.

For the arm holder, you will need to use your modeling skills as a lot of the details are created by hand. Roll out 5½ oz of the gray icing fairly thickly to ¼ inch and cut out two circles with the cutters: the first about 2½ inches and the second a bit smaller. Roll a cylinder to about 1 inch long and about 1¼ inches wide and model a hollow to create the arm holder (step 5). Use an icing tip to make indentations imitating screws (step 5). When all the elements are dry, mix edible silver dust with decorating alcohol and paint the arm, arm holder, and arm head. Allow to dry.

Make the record

Roll out the black icing to about ¼ inch thick and 8 inches wide. Place the 7-inch cake board on top and cut around it with a pizza wheel or a clean paring knife, making sure not to stretch the icing.

Roll out the red icing to about ⅛ inch thick and cut out a circle with a 2-inch diameter circle cutter. Place in the center of the record with a dab of water. Use a piece of the wooden dowel to make the hole in the center of the record. To create the central point in the turntable, roll a piece of gray icing into a cone with a flat base and paint silver. Leave the record and the cone to dry.

For the record grooves glaze the black icing while it is still soft, using a pastry brush (step 5).

Assemble the cake

Place the record onto the turntable and adhere with some water, then use a pastry brush and piping gel to gel the top of the record.

Adhere the silver central piece with piping gel or water, taking care not to smudge.

Place the arm holder at the top right corner of the cake. Adhere together with royal icing, and use more royal icing to stick on the arm, positioning the needle on the record (step 6).

1. Cover the cake.

2. Make the turntable and position on the cake.

3. Make the knobs and controls.

4. Place the controls on the cake.

5. Make the record and the arm.

6. Add the finishing touches.

1

2

This cake is sure to amaze anyone who loves color and make-up. Here, you'll be making your own template and make-up brushes, painting and creating a border.

Make-up box cake

Materials
8-inch square cake
7 tablespoons syrup
3 lb 5 oz ganache
3 lb 5 oz mauve icing (cake)
7 oz black icing (palette)
1½ oz black icing (brushes)
¾ oz pink icing (eyeshadow)
¾ oz aqua icing (eyeshadow)
¾ oz blue icing (eyeshadow)
¾ oz green icing (eyeshadow)
¾ oz yellow icing (eyeshadow)
¾ oz red icing (blush)
¾ oz hot pink icing (blush)
¾ oz orange icing (blush)
¾ oz brown icing (brush)
1 lb 5 oz white icing (board)
Edible silver and lustre dust

Equipment
8-inch square board (set-up)
14-inch square board (display)
7-inch square board
Waxed cardboard (stencil)
Ganaching tools (page 14)
Large and small rolling pins
Pasta machine
Plastic sheets
Small kitchen knife or paring knife
Flexi-scraper
Smoothers
Set of circle cutters
Ruler
Paintbrushes
Scissors

1

2

1. Cover the cake and mark the decorative border.

2. Position the palette with a dab of water.

3. Paint the border and cut the circles in the palette.

4. Roll out the make-up colors and place them on the palette.

5. Make the make-up brush and applicator.

6. Cover the board and add the finishing touches.

3

4

5

6

Use a small knife to mark the brush lines to achieve a realistic look.

Prepare the cake
Follow the instructions on how to prepare and ganache a square cake (page 39).

Cover the cake
Roll out the mauve icing to ⅛ inch thick. Follow the instructions on how to cover a square cake (page 46).

For the decorative border, and while the icing is still soft, use a ruler to mark around the top of the sides of the cake (step 1). Mix together edible silver dust and decorating alcohol and paint the border with a paintbrush.

For the palette, use a 7-inch square cake board as a template. Roll out the black icing to ⅛ inch thick and cut out a 7-inch square. Place on the top of the cake with a dab of water around the edges only (step 2).

Make the make-up brush holder
Enlarge the template (page 186) on a photocopier, trace on waxed paper and cut it out. While the icing is still soft use the template to stamp the make-up brush holder into the cake. Be careful, you only get one chance to place this correctly. The indent does not need to be too deep.

Use a medium or large circle cutter to cut out four circles in the make-up palette and a small circle cutter to cut the three circles along the edge. Peel away the black icing (step 3).

Make the colors
Make the pink, aqua, blue, green, red, yellow, and hot pink icings (or any colors you have chosen) and roll them out to ⅛ inch thick with a rolling pin or pasta machine.

Use the same circle cutters you used to create the palette to cut out the make-up colors, then cut two of them in half and mix and match (step 4). Brush lustre dust on the colors to enhance the look of the make-up.

Repeat these steps for the blush, using red, hot pink, and orange icing. Place the make-up on the palette with a dab of water to secure them. Smooth over with a flexi-scraper.

Make the brush and applicator
For the brush, roll out ¾ oz of the black icing to ¼-inch thick and 4½-inch long sausage, tapered at one end. Use a bit of the brown icing about the size of a pea and shape it into a teardrop. Flatten it to get a brush-like shape then mark the brush lines. Glue the brush to the stick. Paint the front of the brush in edible silver dust mixed with decorating alcohol (page 61).

For the applicator, roll out the remaining black icing to ¼-inch thick and 3¼-inch long sausage, tapered at both ends. Use a small amount of white icing (left-over from the board) and roll two balls. Flatten the balls to a teardrop and then stick on both ends of the black stick (step 5).

Cover the display board
Follow the instructions on how to cover a board, using either method (page 48).

Assemble the cake
Place the cake on the board and decorate with the make-up brushes and products.

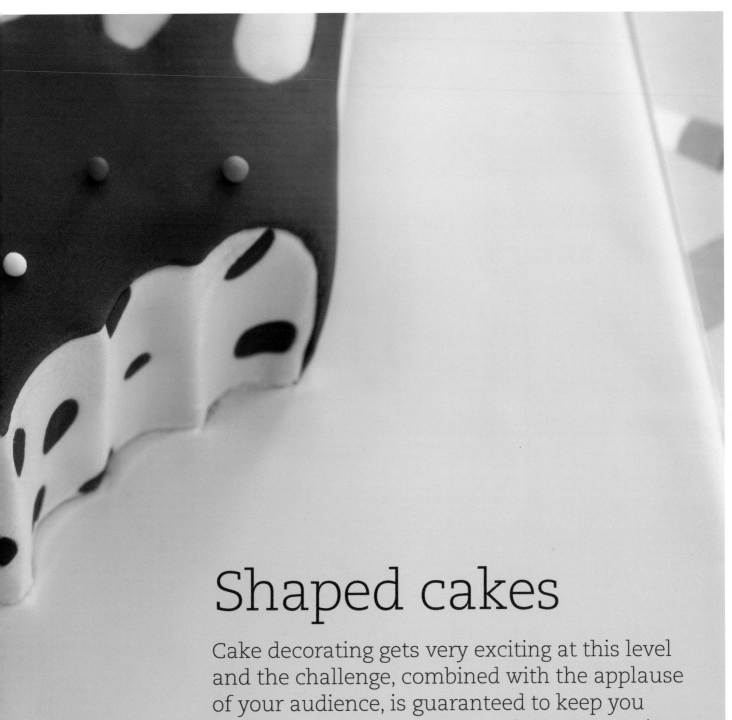

Shaped cakes

Cake decorating gets very exciting at this level
and the challenge, combined with the applause
of your audience, is guaranteed to keep you
hooked. With most of these cakes, once you've
mastered the basic concept, you can adapt the
colors and designs to suit any occasion.

This is a truly versatile design and, once you've mastered the shape, it's really only limited by your imagination. Use the flag of a favorite sports team for Father's Day, or that of a country to celebrate a special trip.

Flag cake

Materials
8-inch square cake
10 tablespoons syrup
3 lb 5 oz ganache
2 lb 10 oz light blue icing (cake)
1 lb 9 oz light blue icing (board)
5½ oz orange icing (strips)
5½ oz pink icing (strips)
5½ oz blue icing (strips)
5½ oz yellow icing (strips)
7 oz brown icing (flagpole)
Edible glitter in pink
10½ oz white icing (tassels)
Decorating alcohol
Royal icing
Edible gold dust
Cornstarch

Equipment
16-inch square cake board (display)
6 x 8 inch rectangular DIY board
Ganaching tools (page 14)
Large and small rolling pins
Pasta machine
Plastic sheets
Small kitchen knife or paring knife
Flexi-scraper
Plastic scraper
Ruler
Pizza wheel
Smoothers
Paintbrushes

1

2

1. Shape and ganache the cake.

2. Cut out the wave on one-half of the cake and flip over onto the other half.

3. Cover the cake and board.

4. Add the glitter and roll out the flagpole and ball.

5. Make the rope and tassels.

6. Attach the flagpole, rope and tassels to the cake and board.

3

4

5

6

Mix gold dust with decorating alcohol and paint the tassels.

For the letters on the cake use a font you like and trace it on before you apply the glitter.

avoid staining it. Keep the strips covered with plastic.

Moisten the surface of the cake with a dab of water and place the strips on top, making sure the strips are as close together as possible (step 3). Manipulate the icing by pushing it to make it sit exactly on the cake. Quickly run the flexi-scraper over to smooth it. Using a sharp paring knife, trim the top to sit neatly at the sides (step 3).

Roll out the flagpole
Knead the brown icing to a pliable dough. On a work surface lightly dusted with cornstarch, roll the brown icing into a 10 x 1 inch sausage. Use the cake smoother to roll it evenly (page 62). Place the flagpole with a little dab of water on the board next to the flag (step 6). With the remaining brown icing, roll a ball in the size of a walnut and place it on the top of the flagpole (steps 4+6).

Write with edible glitter
For the DIY template, find a "font" you like and make your own template (page 57). Stencil the lettering onto the cake. Using a fine paintbrush, trace over the lettering with syrup, sprinkle edible glitter onto the syrupy lettering, and press gently to stick the glitter to the syrup. Let the glitter dry, then gently blow away any excess.

Make the rope and tassels
Use half the amount of the white icing for the tassels (page 55). For the rope, roll out two rolls (page 62) of the remaining white icing to 24 inches in length and then twist together (step 5). Brush the rope and tassels with the edible gold dust (page 61). Allow to dry before attaching the rope and tassels onto the board and around the flagpole (step 6).

Shape and ganache the cake
Trim 2 inches from the side of the 8-inch square and stick to a now shorter side with ganache, to get a 6 x 10 inch rectangle (step 1).

Using a long serrated knife, cut a moon shape from one half of your rectangle, but don't cut deeper than one-third of the cake's depth. Flip the piece over onto the flat piece of the uncut rectangle and stick it on with ganache (step 2). Apply a little bit of ganache to the cake to seal the crumbs, and make sure the flag shape is perfect, before following the instructions on how to ganache a 12 x 8 inch rectangular cake (page 40). Allow the ganache to set completely.

Cover the cake
Knead the blue icing to a pliable dough. Roll out to ⅛ inch thick and follow the instructions on how to cover a shaped cake (page 47). Let sit for a couple of hours.

Cover the display board
Follow the instructions on how to cover a board, using either method (page 48). If you prefer to put the cake on a differently covered board, make sure the cake sits on a set-up board.

Make and arrange the flag strips
Roll out the colored icing with a pasta machine, or with a rolling pin, to ⅛ inch thick. Measure your cake and cut enough strips in different colors and widths to cover your cake, using a pizza wheel and a ruler. Make sure not to get any cornflour on top of the icing, to

This is smart, stylish, and always a hit with adults and children alike. If you want to add more color, pipe colored dragees on the chocolate icing.

Ice-cream cake

Materials
8-inch square cake
7 tablepsoons syrup
2 lb 10 oz ganache
2¼ lb pink icing (cake)
1 lb 2 oz brown icing (chocolate dribbles)
1 lb 9 oz white icing (board)
7 oz caramel icing (ice-cream stick)
Cornstarch

Equipment
12 x 8 inch rectangular board (display)
Ganaching tools (page 14)
Large and small rolling pins
Pasta machine
Plastic sheets
Cranked palette knife
Plastic scraper
Flexi-scraper
Smoothers
Circle cutter (3¼ inches)
Scissors
Paintbrushes

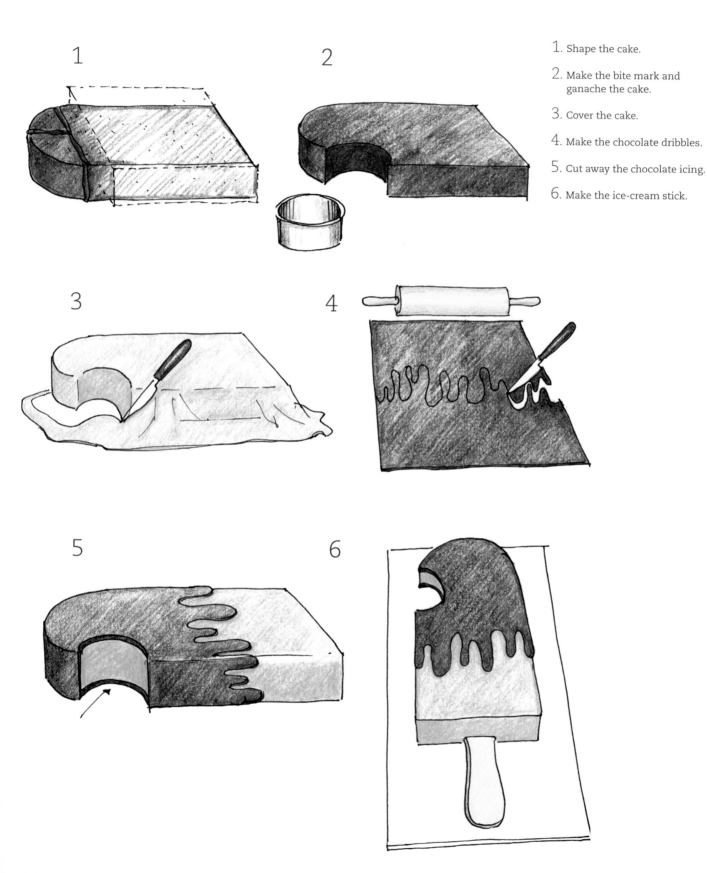

1. Shape the cake.

2. Make the bite mark and ganache the cake.

3. Cover the cake.

4. Make the chocolate dribbles.

5. Cut away the chocolate icing.

6. Make the ice-cream stick.

You can vary the design by adding more bite marks, using a slightly smaller circle cutter (design on page 136).

Shape the cake

Enlarge the ice-cream template (page 189) on a photocopier. Trace the template onto a sheet of waxed paper and cut out.

Follow the instructions on how to cut a square into a rectangular cake (page 40).

Place the template on top of the rectangular cake and, with a small serrated knife, cut around it, making sure to keep the knife vertical to maintain a right-angle.

Place the cake on the board, leaving enough room for the ice-cream stick.

Make the bite mark and ganache the cake

Using the large circle cutter, cut out the bite mark (step 2). Follow the instructions on how to ganache a square cake (page 39). Allow to set before covering.

Cover the cake

Knead the pink icing to a pliable dough and roll out to ⅛ inch thick. Follow the instructions on how to cover a shaped cake (page 47).

Try to get the square edge of the ice-cream sharp and leave the sides slightly rounded. Allow time for the icing to dry (preferably overnight) before continuing.

Make the chocolate dribbles

Enlarge the template for the ice-cream dribbles (page 189). Trace it onto waxed paper and cut out. Roll out the brown icing to ⅛ inch thick and large enough to cover half of the cake. Place the template on the icing, then cut out the dribbles using a paring knife (step 4).

Dampen the cake where the brown icing is to go with a little water. Smooth the icing with a flexi-scraper and trim the bottom. Cut away the brown icing at the bite mark to expose the pink icing underneath and smooth the edges.

Cover the display board

Knead the white icing to a pliable dough and roll out to ⅛ inch thick. Follow the instructions on how to cover the board around the cake (page 51).

Make the ice-cream stick

Enlarge the ice-cream stick template (page 189) on a photocopier. Trace on waxed paper and cut it out.

Roll out the caramel icing to about ½ inch thick and mold into the shape of an ice-cream stick, using the template as a guide. Brush a line of water on the correct position on the board and lay the stick over it (step 6).

This is a great cake for beach lovers, surfers, or just to celebrate the start of summer. The colors and flowers are easily changed to something more masculine if need be (try fish, suns, or stars). Here, you'll be introduced to using non-edible materials as decoration, such as the acetate strap.

Flip flop cake

Materials
8-inch square cake
7 tablespoons syrup
3 lb 5 oz ganache
2 lb 10 oz orange icing (cake and flower centers)
10½ oz yellow icing (top layer)
Wooden skewer
3¾ oz pink icing (flowers)
Pink royal icing
Clear A4 plastic acetate
Double-sided sticky tape
5½ oz royal icing
⅓ cup raw sugar
Coral brown food coloring

Equipment
14 x 20 inch rectangular board (display)
Waxed cardboard (DIY board)
Ganaching tools (page 14)
Scissors
Large and small rolling pins
Pasta machine
Plastic sheets
Cranked palette knife
Flexi-scraper
Plastic scraper
Smoothers
Pizza wheel
Paintbrushes
Wire cutters (secateurs)
Large blossom cutter
No. 2 icing tip
Icing bag

Shape and ganache the flip flop
Enlarge the flip flop template (page 187) on a photocopier. Trace the template onto a sheet of waxed paper and cut out, then convert into a DIY board for the cake, using waxed cardboard (page 62).

Follow the instructions on how to cut and shape a 12 x 8 inch rectangular cake (page 40).

Place the flip flop template on top of the cake (step 1, page 149) and use a small serrated knife to cut around it, making sure to hold the knife straight down to maintain a right-angle. Build up the shape of the flip flop with trim-offs sandwiched together with ganache. Smooth the shaped cake with ganache (page 41).

Tip: Focus on the sides of the cake before finishing the top.

Cover the flip flop

Knead 2¼ lb of the orange icing to a pliable dough and roll out to ⅛ inch thick. Follow the instructions on how to cover a shaped cake (page 47), (step 2).

Apply the top layer

Use a rolling pin to roll out the yellow icing to about ⅛ inch thick. Place the flip flop template on top and cut around it with a pizza wheel or small knife. Gently lift the icing and place it onto the shaped cake to check the dimensions are correct; the icing should just overlap the sides. If it is not an accurate fit, manipulate the icing by stretching or pushing it.

Using a damp brush, apply a thin layer of syrup all over the cake. With the same brush, gently lift the icing around the sides and brush the bottom, then stick the icing onto the cake with a small amount of syrup.

Prepare the toe area

Insert a wooden skewer into the toe area; leave 1½ inches of the skewer above the cake. Clip off the excess with wire cutters or use a pair of strong scissors.

Roll out a small piece of orange icing in a pasta machine to about ⅛ inch thick. Cut out a small strip of 2 x ¾ inches. Wrap the strip around the sides of the skewer and secure with a dab of water (step 3). Mark the position of the straps with a sharp knife about two-thirds of the way down from the top of the flip flop on each side.

Make the flower decoration

Roll out the pink icing and 3½ oz of the orange icing in a pasta machine to ⅛ inch thick. Using a small flower cutter, cut out flowers in the pink icing, and then with a no. 2 icing tip, cut out the same amount of circles

Roughly apply the sand icing with a palette knife around the flip flop on the board to create the beach impression.

in the orange icing. Stick a circle on the center of each flower and place the flowers randomly on the flip flop, keeping one flower aside for the strap.

Re-knead the icing and roll out again. Using a cutter, or a small knife, cut an oval for the label from the orange icing. Fill a icing bag with pink royal icing and with a very small tip pipe out the name onto the oval shape. Allow it to dry and then place it onto the flip flop, brushing it with a little water to make it stick.

Make the straps

Cut two acetate strips to the desired width. Stick one end of an acetate strip to the top of the skewer with double-sided sticky tape and push the other end into the marked area (step 4). Use double-sided tape to press a second strip on top of the first one.

Roll out the remaining orange icing in the pasta machine, or by hand, to ⅛ inch thick. Cut four strips the same size as the acetate strips and cover the icing strips with a

sheet of plastic.

Brush syrup on the acetate strip and cover it with the icing on both sides (page 60), but leave about 1½ inches of the acetate without the icing. Push the uncovered piece of strip into the cake, using the template for the correct position. Repeat this with the other strip. Support the straps with tissue paper until completely dry, then remove (step 5). Stick the remaining flower onto the joining line with a dab of water.

Cover the display board and apply the sand

Follow the instructions on how to cover a board around the cake (page 51), making sure the joining line is at the back of the flip flop. Apply the sand icing onto the board and around the flip flop, using a palette knife. See instructions on how to make the sand (page 61). Decorate the board.

1. Use the template to cut the shape from a rectangular cake.

2. Cover the flip flop in orange icing.

3. Cover the flip flop with yellow icing and mark holes for straps. Insert skewer and trim, then wrap sides with orange icing.

4. Stick acetate strips to the skewer and cover with orange icing.

5. Position flowers and support the straps with tissue paper until dry.

6. Cover the board and decorate with sand icing.

Bake, decorate, blast off! This bold and bright cake will help you perfect your molding of rounded shapes. The decorations are all created from cut-outs and templates, and you will be painting with edible silver dust to add sparkle.

Rocket cake

Materials
8-inch square cake
7 tablespoons syrup
2 lb 10 oz ganache
2¼ lb orange icing (cake)
1 lb 9 oz black icing (board)
3½ oz green icing (door and stars)
1¾ oz blue icing (window)
14 oz red icing (nose and wings)
1¾ oz grey icing (trim and details)
4¼ oz yellow icing (strips)
1¾ oz black icing (alien)
Edible dust in silver
Decoratoring alcohol
Golden dragrees

Equipment
16-inch round board (display)
Waxed cardboard (DIY board)
Ganaching tools (page 14)
Scissors
Large and small rolling pins
Pasta machine
Plastic sheets
Small kitchen or paring knife
Flexi-scraper
Plastic scraper
Smoother
Paintbrushes
Set of circle cutters
Star cutter
Stitching tool
No. 1 icing tip
Pizza wheel
Frilling tool
Clear plastic drinking straw
Cotton wool

Shape and ganache the cake
Enlarge the rocket template (page 188) on a photocopier. Trace the template on waxed paper and cut it out. Follow the instructions on how to shape a square into a 12 x 8 inch rectangular cake (page 40).

Place the template on top of the cake and with a small serrated knife cut out the shape of the rocket (step 1, page 152). Use a serrated knife to taper the front of the rocket to a very low point; keep the top highest part and the middle part about 4 to 6 inches high. Use the cake trim-offs to give the rocket its half-round shape, sticking it on with ganache. Keep cutting and sticking until it looks perfectly balanced from every angle. Brush the cake with syrup all over, and then ganache (step 2, page 152). Allow to set.

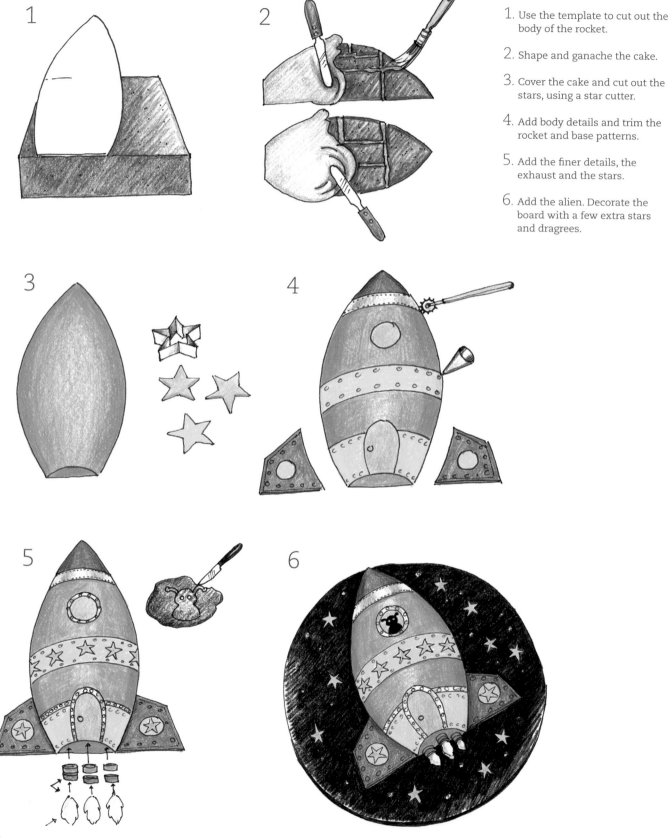

1. Use the template to cut out the body of the rocket.

2. Shape and ganache the cake.

3. Cover the cake and cut out the stars, using a star cutter.

4. Add body details and trim the rocket and base patterns.

5. Add the finer details, the exhaust and the stars.

6. Add the alien. Decorate the board with a few extra stars and dragrees.

The smart use of drinking straws and cotton wool creates the effect of smoke coming out of the "starting" engine.

Create a DIY board
Trace the rocket template you made earlier onto waxed cardboard. Cut it out to make the DIY board to put underneath the cake.

Cover the cake
Knead the orange icing to a pliable dough and roll out to ⅛ inch thick. Follow the instructions on how to cover a shaped cake (page 47). Keep the edges sharp and trim the icing very neatly at the base (step 3).

Cover the display board
Knead the black icing to a pliable dough and roll out to ⅛ inch thick. Follow the general instructions on how to cover the board, using either method (page 48).

Make the door and window
Roll out 1¾ oz of each of the green and blue icing to ⅛ inch thick. Using the template, cut out the door and use a medium circle cutter to cut out the window. Cover the shapes with plastic to prevent drying out.

Make the trims and details
For the nose, roll out ¾ oz of the red icing to ⅛ inch thick. Brush the nose area with a little water and place the red icing over it, making sure to align it properly. Cut away the excess icing with a knife.

For the strips, roll out about 2¾ oz of the yellow icing and 1½ oz of the gray icing to ⅛ inch thick. Cut two yellow strips and one gray strip of 1¼ inches wide and long enough to cover the rocket from side to side. Brush the rocket with a little water and stick on the strips. Place the door template on the bottom strip and cut out a gap. Stick the door and the window on the rocket with a dab of water (steps 3+4).

For the stars, roll out the remaining green icing and the remaining yellow icing to ⅛ inch thick and cut out 17 stars using a star cutter (step 3). Stick them onto the rocket and board with a dab of water. Save two stars for the wings.

For the silver trims, roll out the remaining gray icing to ⅛ inch thick.

Using a circle cutter, cut out a circle and with a smaller circle cutter cut away the inner circle. Stick this over the window to get the window frame. For the door, roll a very thin grey sausage. Dampen the edge of the door and stick the thin sausage around the door. Use a stitching tool, icing tip and frilling tool to create effects (step 4). Mix the silver dust with decorating alcohol and paint the grey icing (page 61). Allow to dry.

Make the finishing touches
For the wings, roll out the remaining red icing to about ¼ inch thick. Use the template to cut out the wings with a pizza wheel or a small knife. Stick the wings onto the board right next to the rocket with a little bit of water.

For the engines, roll a small amount of left-over orange icing (about the size of a hazelnut) into a ball, then mold it to a disc between your index finger and thumb. Do the same with the left-over red icing, but make the disc a bit smaller. Repeat to make three of each. Stick the orange discs on the red discs (step 5). Brush the end of the rocket with a little water and stick the engines, orange side down, on it (step 6).

For the smoke, cut an extra large clear drinking straw into three 2-inch long pieces. Poke a little cotton wool in the end of the straw. Repeat this with the other two straws. Stick the straws into the engines so that only the smoke is seen.

For the alien, roll out the black icing to ⅛ inch thick. Trace an alien DIY template onto waxed paper and cut it out. Place the template on the black icing and cut around it with a small knife (step 5). Stick your alien character onto the window with a dab of water (step 6).

Stick the dragrees around the rocket on the board with a little dab of water.

Perfect for any fashionistas you know. Once you've mastered the boot you can change the shape to make any shoe you like. This cake introduces you to hand painting and is a great opportunity to let your imagination run wild.

Boot cake

Materials
8-inch square cake
3 lb 5 oz ganache
7 tablespoons syrup
3 lb 5 oz ivory icing (cake)
1 lb 2 oz caramel icing (sole and heel)
Black food coloring
Brown food coloring
Decorating alcohol
14 oz orange icing (bow)

Equipment
12 x 20 inch rectangular board (display)
Ganaching tools (page 14)
Large and small rolling pins
Pasta machine
Plastic sheets
Small kitchen knife or paring knife
Cranked palette knife
Flexi-scraper
Smoothers
Plastic scraper
Paintbrushes

Cover the display board
Follow the instructions on how to cover the whole board (page 49). Allow to dry and harden. (You will be placing the semi-finished cake onto the board.)

Shape the cake
Follow the instructions on how to cut a square cake into a 12 x 8 inch rectangular shape (page 40). Enlarge the boot template (page 186) on a photocopier. Trace the template onto waxed paper and cut out. Once the cake is joined and filled, place the template on top and cut around it. Use the trim-offs to build the shape (step 2, page 156). Smooth the ganache and allow to set.

1. Use the template to cut the boot from the cake.

2. Bind the cake with syrup and cover with ganache.

3. Cover the cake.

4. Apply the sole and make the high heel.

5. Paint the pattern on the boot and make the bow.

6. Place the bow around the ankle of the boot.

The striking color of the bow adds a great contrast to the animal print.

Cover the cake
Measure the boot and brush lightly with syrup. Knead the ivory icing to a pliable dough, then roll out to ⅛ inch thick. Cover the cake with the icing (step 3), following the instructions on how to cover a shaped cake (page 47).

Apply the sole and make the heel
Knead 10½ oz of the caramel icing to a pliable consistency and roll out to ⅛ inch thick. Roughly cut the icing in the shape of the sole and stick it underneath the boot. Using a sharp small knife, trim the edges.

Mold a heel out of the remaining caramel icing. Measure the distance between the sole and where it will sit to find the right height for the heel. Using your fingers, create the shape of the cone first, then mold it into the shape of a heel. Use the back of a knife to decorate the heel. Allow it to dry, then stick it onto the board underneath the sole with a dab of water (step 4).

Paint the pattern
Combine the brown food coloring with the decorating alcohol. Paint the brown spots in random size and pattern onto the boot, starting from the center and working to the sides and up and down.

Combine the black food coloring with the cake decorating alcohol and paint around the brown spots to create an animal skin pattern (step 5). Work quickly, as your paints will dry out fast (page 61).

Make the bow
Knead 12 oz of the orange icing to a pliable dough. Follow the instructions on how to make a bow (page 58).

Place the bow
Roll out the remaining orange icing to ⅛ inch thick.

For the anklet ribbon, cut a strip of icing to 6 x ¾ inches, and place it onto the boot around the ankle with a thin line of water. Trim the excess strip.

For the ribbon "tails", cut two fat rectangles in the same width as your bow and about 2 inches long. Cut a V-shape out of one end of each tail and place it underneath the bow. Place the semi-dry bow on top and stick with a dab of water (steps 5+6). Allow to dry.

Tip: For a puffy bow, place some tissue paper or cotton wool in the loops and remove when the icing has dried.

Three-dimensional cakes

We do, of course, know that all cakes are three-dimensional, but this is what we call our spectacular sculpted, modelled creations. They're fun, fantastic, and obviously a bit more tricky to make (which is why they're at the end of the book). Don't be nervous — you have all the techniques perfected by now.

You've got the skills now, so reach for the sky. This cake is a great introduction to sculpting. The airplane is cartoonish rather than realistic, so keep everything rounded and child-like.

Airplane cake

Material
8-inch square cake
7 tablespoons syrup
3 lb 5 oz ganache
2 lb 7 oz white icing (cake and clouds)
2¼ lb sky blue icing (board)
3½ oz black icing (strips and eyes)
1¾ oz grey icing (nose)
10½ oz light blue icing (wings and tail)
3½ oz watermelon-colored icing (strips)
2 toothpicks
Black food coloring
Decorating alcohol

Equipment
18-inch round board (display)
Waxed cardboard (DIY board)
Ganaching tools (page 14)
Scissors
Large and small rolling pins
Pasta machine
Plastic sheets
Cranked palette knife
Flexi-scraper
Smoother
Plastic scraper
Frilling tool
Set of circle cutters
Pizza wheel
Paintbrushes

Prepare and shape the cake
Enlarge the airplane template (page 186) on a photocopier. Trace the template onto a sheet of waxed cardboard and cut it out. Follow the instructions on how to make a square cake into a rectangular cake (page 40). Then read the instructions on how to ganache a shaped cake (page 41). Once the cake is filled, place the template on top and cut around it (step 1, page 162). Use the trim-offs to build the front of the airplane (step 2). The front part is almost as rounded as a ball. Taper the tail part downwards. Ganache the cake and place it on the final board (step 2, page 162). Allow to set.

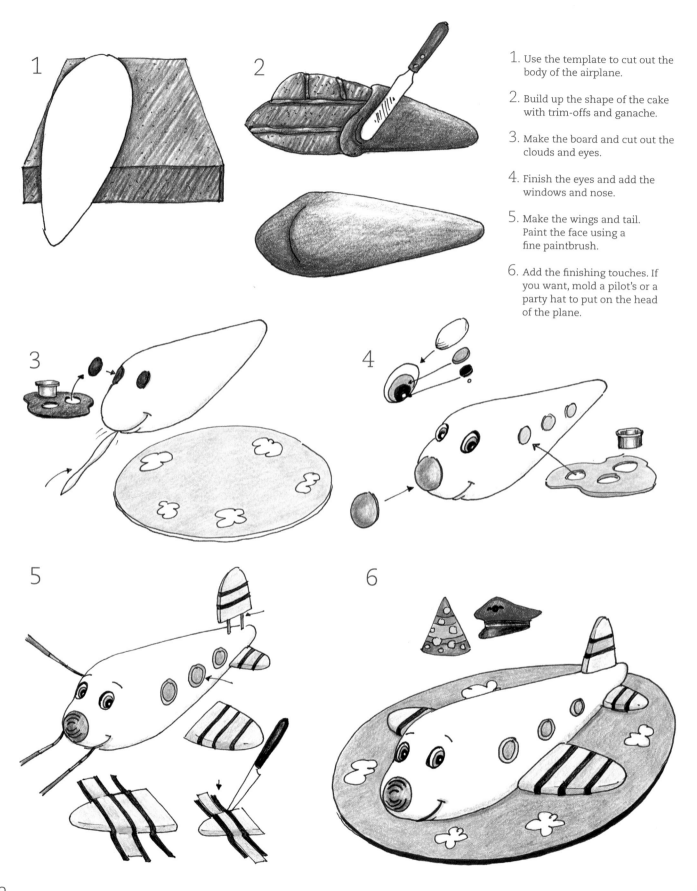

1. Use the template to cut out the body of the airplane.

2. Build up the shape of the cake with trim-offs and ganache.

3. Make the board and cut out the clouds and eyes.

4. Finish the eyes and add the windows and nose.

5. Make the wings and tail. Paint the face using a fine paintbrush.

6. Add the finishing touches. If you want, mold a pilot's or a party hat to put on the head of the plane.

Wrap strips in different colors and widths around the wings to create a cartoon look.

Cover the cake
Knead 2¼ lb of the white icing to a pliable dough and roll out to ⅛ inch thick. Follow the instructions on how to cover a shaped cake (page 47).

Cover the display board
Knead 1¾ lb of the sky blue icing to a pliable dough and roll out to ⅛ inch thick. Follow the instructions on how to cover a board around the cake (page 51).

Make the clouds
Draw your own cloud templates in two different sizes. Roll out the remaining white icing to ⅛ inch thick. Place the template on top and cut around it. Stick the clouds on the board with a little water (step 3).

Make the face
For the mouth and eyes, while the icing is still soft use a frilling tool to indent the mouth at the front of the plane (step 3). Press your thumb into the cake to indent the eyes.

Roll out small amounts of black, sky blue, and left-over white icing to ⅛ inch thick and cover it with plastic. Cut out two black 1 x ½ inch ovals,

using either a round cutter and then stretching the circles slightly, or by cutting freehand. Cut out two smaller white ovals and blue ovals and even smaller ovals in black (step 4). Finish with two tiny white ovals. With a little water stick the ovals on the cake, starting with a large black oval followed by white, blue, black, and white ovals reducing in size.

For the nose, roll out the gray icing to ⅛ inch thick. Cut out a disc using a 2-inch circle cutter. Stick the nose ono the cake with a little water (step 4).

Make the windows
Use a 1¼-inch circle cutter to indent three windows on each side of the plane. Roll out some of the sky blue icing to ⅛ inch, and then use the circle cutter to cut out six discs for the windows. Stick three windows on each side of the plane with a little water (step 4). Make two long, thin rolls from the light blue icing and the watermelon icing. Cut into six lengths long enough to go around the windows, and stick them on with a little water (step 5).

Make the wings and tail
Roll out the remaining light blue icing to ⅝ inch thick. Use the template (page 186) to cut out the four wings and tail with a small sharp knife. Smooth the outer edges of the pieces with your fingers, but not where they join the plane. Roll out the remaining black and watermelon-colored icing to ⅛ inch thick. Using a pizza wheel, or a small sharp knife, cut out strips in different widths long enough to cover the wings. Stick them onto the wings with a little water and trim (step 5). Stick wings onto the board next to the plane with a little water (step 5). Poke two toothpicks into the tail from underneath, at the joining edge. Stick the tail onto the airplane with a little water (step 5).

Paint the face
Mix black food coloring and a drop of decorating alcohol. Paint the eyebrows, mouth, and details on the nose (step 5).

Every time we create a "food" cake at Planet Cake, people respond with rapturous applause and child-like wonder. You'll need an especially firm cake here, such as the chocolate mud cake. Modeling the icing is one of the most enjoyable cake-decorating skills to master.

Barbecue cake

Materials
9-inch round cake
7 tablespoons syrup
3 lb 5 oz ganache
1 oz black icing (coal)
7 oz gray icing (coal)
1¾ oz orange icing (flame)
1¾ oz black icing (flame)
1¾ oz red icing (flame)
2¼ lb red icing (cake)
1 lb 9 oz green icing (board)
3½ oz black royal icing
3½ oz caramel icing (handle)
Black, caramel, yellow, brown, red, and blue food colorings
10½ oz white icing (meat)
¾ oz green icing (green pepper)
¾ oz red icing (red pepper)
8 toothpicks
Edible silver dust
Decorating alcohol
Glaze

Equipment
9-inch round board (set-up)
5-inch round board (set-up)
14-inch round board (display)
Ganaching tools (page 14)
Large and small rolling pins
Pasta machine
Plastic sheets
Cranked palette knife
Flexi-scraper
Smoother
Plastic scraper
Pizza wheel
Frilling tool
Ruler
Small kitchen knife or paring knife
Kitchen scourer
Icing bag
No. 3 icing tip
Paintbrush

Prepare and shape the cake
Follow the instructions on how to prepare and ganache a round cake (page 38), but only fill the layers. Once it is filled, start shaping the cake by placing it on a turntable with the 9-inch board on the bottom and the 5-inch board on the top, as a guide for tapering. Stick the trim-offs to the cake with ganache to build up the inverted bowl shape. Keep in mind as you are shaping the cake that it is upside down (step 1, page 166).

Turn the cake, roughly ganache and let it set, preferably overnight (step 2, page 166).

Make the coal
Partially mix some black icing into the gray icing to give it a streaky effect (page 61). Roll out the gray icing to ¼ inch thick and large

1. Use two round cake boards as guides to shape the cake.

2. Mold the cake into the inverted bowl shape with ganache and trim-offs. Turn the cake over and leave to dry overnight.

3. Make the grill and cover the sides of the barbecue.

4. Add the handles and pipe the meat grill.

5. Mold and paint the meat.

6. Assemble the barbecue and add the finishing touches.

To get the barbecued effect for the meat, mark charred lines with the back of a knife and paint the lines with brown food color.

enough to cover the top of the cake. Place pieces of orange, black, and red icing randomly on the gray icing. Roll out again with the sprinkled pieces on top to about ⅛ inch thick. Using a 9-inch cake board as a template, cut the icing with a pizza wheel. Brush the top of the cake with syrup and place the icing on top. Manipulate the icing to fit (step 3). Allow it to dry.

For the grill rack, use a ruler to mark the lines every ¾ inch, and create the grooves with a frilling tool or the back of a paring knife.

Cover the cake
Brush the side of the cake (not the top) with syrup. Measure the height and circumference of the cake and roll out the red icing to ⅛ inch thick. Follow the instructions on how to cover a shaped cake (page 47). Press the icing against the side (step 3). Put the 9-inch cake board on top of the cake and cut around the board, making sure not to damage the charcoal base. Lift the red icing up, smooth the edges with the flexi-scraper and trim at the base. Push the icing inwards with a frilling tool.

Cover the display board
Roll out the green icing to ⅛ inch thick and follow the instructions on how to cover the board (page 48), using either method. While the icing is still soft press a kitchen scourer in the icing to create a grass texture.

Make the grill
Fill an icing bag with black royal icing. With a no. 3 icing tip, pipe along the grooves on the grill top (step 4). Mix edible silver dust with decorating alcohol and paint the grill.

Tip: If you are not confident piping using the icing bag, roll thin black sausages and place them along the grooves with a dab of water and paint when dry.

Make the handles
Roll out 2¾ oz of the caramel icing and cut two rectangles about ½ inch thick, 3¼ inches long, and ¾ inch wide. In addition, make four small, round ½-inch thick discs.

When the handles are semidry, poke two toothpicks into each side of the cake and skewer one disc on each toothpick using royal icing as glue. Stack the handles on top of the toothpicks and discs (step 4).

Make the meat and the kebab
To make the kebab meat, mix a little yellow, brown, and blue food coloring into white icing and roll into a long brick shape. Cut into slices using a paring knife in a sawing motion to get a meat effect. Use a paintbrush to lightly paint the pieces with brown food coloring mixed with decorating alcohol to exaggerate the color.

For the peppers, roll out the green and red icings to about ¹⁄₁₆ inch thick. Cut into squares, then curl slightly for a natural look. Use a bit of brown food coloring mixed with decorating alcohol and paint marks on the edges for a barbecued effect.

When partially dry, place the meat and pieces of pepper together to look like a kebab and poke toothpicks in the end to imitate skewers (step 5, see **Note** page 11).

For the chicken drumsticks, add drops of brown and yellow food coloring to the white icing and roll into a ball. Mold into a large teardrop then shape into a drumstick. Add skin texture with a grater. Mark charred lines with the back of a paring knife and paint the lines brown with undiluted food coloring. Partially paint the leg with brown food coloring mixed with alcohol to give it a cooked effect.

For the sausage, mix brown and red into the white icing, then mold into two balls and roll into sausages. Bend slightly. Mark charred lines with the back of a paring knife and paint them with undiluted brown food coloring. Mix brown and red food coloring with decorating alcohol and brush the sausages.

Assemble the barbecue
Stick the kebabs on top of the barbecue with royal icing then add the drumsticks and sausages. Follow the instructions on how to glaze (page 54). Glaze the meat on the

This stunning cake is always the star of any party. While the giant cupcake looks incredibly professional, the majority of energy is required for perfecting the dome shape rather than decorating.

Giant cupcake

Material
8-inch square cake
7 tablespoons syrup
3 lb 5 oz ganache
3½ oz white icing (separator)
3 wooden skewers
1 lb brown icing (cake)
10½ oz blue icing ("paper liner")
10½ oz white icing (icing)
3½ oz red royal icing (sprinkles)
3½ oz blue royal icing (sprinkles)
1½ oz red icing (cherry)
1 lb 9 oz white icing (board)
Glaze
Green florist tape

Equipment
5-inch round board (set-up)
7-inch round board (set-up)
14-inch round board (display)
Ganaching tools (page 14)
Large and small rolling pins
Pasta machine
Plastic sheets
Cranked palette knife
Flexi-scraper
Smoother
Plastic scraper
Small serrated knife
Pizza wheel
Ruler
Scissors
No. 2 icing tip
Icing bag
Frilling tool
Small wire covered with green
   florist tape

Prepare and shape the cake
For the base, cut the cake in three even layers and sandwich them together with ganache. Follow the instructions on how to prepare and ganache (pages 38–39).

Center the 5-inch round cake board on top and the 7-inch round board underneath the square cake, using a dab of ganache to hold them in place (step 1, page 170). Keep in mind as you are working that the cake is upside down.

Use a large serrated knife to taper the cake out towards the base, and a small serrated knife to shave the cake until it looks neat and the top of the cake is 7 inches. Turn the cake right side up (step 2, page 170).

Push in the three wooden skewers within the 5-inch diameter and trim flush with the cake (step 3).

1. Use the different-sized round boards as guides to shape the base of the cupcake.

2. Invert the cake and shape the dome.

3. Use wooden skewers and ganache to shape the dome.

4. Cover the dome with chocolate icing and trim flush with the base. Cover the base and use a wooden skewer to make the 'paper case' decorations.

5. Ice the dome and dot on the colored sprinkles. Make the cherry and glaze.

6. Add the finishing touches.

Devote a bit of time making the cherry to achieve the most realistic shape. The glaze gives the cherry a beautiful glossy finish.

Make the separator and dome

Roll out the white icing to $^1/_{16}$ inch thick using the 7-inch cake board as a template, and cut it out with a pizza wheel. With a dab of ganache, stick the icing on top of the layered cake and stick the cake board on top of the icing.

Build the dome with the trim-offs, using ganache for sticking it on. Keep shaving the dome unil it looks perfectly balanced from every angle (page 41). Stick your cake onto the 5-inch set-up board, ganache and allow it to set.

Cover the cake

Follow the instructions on how to cover a shaped cake (page 47). Measure the circumference and the height of the cake from the top to just below the dome. Brush the area of the dome that will be covered with icing with water or syrup.

Knead the brown icing to a pliable dough and roll it out to about $^1/_8$ inch thick.

Cover the dome and smooth with the flexi-scraper. Trim the icing just below the dome (step 4).

For the "paper liner", measure the circumference and height of the base. Roll out the blue icing to about $^1/_8$ inch thick and large enough to cover the base. Cut into a rectangle. Brush the cake with syrup and wrap the icing around the cake (page 47). Mark the "paper liner" indentations with a barbecue skewer (page 62).

For the icing on the dome, enlarge the template (page 187) on a photocopier. Trace it on waxed paper and cut it out. Measure the area to be covered and brush with syrup. Roll out the white icing to $^1/_8$ inch thick. Put your template on top of the icing and cut it out (step 5). Stick the icing on top of the dome.

Make the sprinkles

Fill an icing bag one-third full with the red royal icing. Using a no. 2 icing tip, dot sprinkles over the dome of the cake. Clean the icing bag and fill with the blue royal icing, then dot sprinkles over the dome.

Make the cherry

Roll the red icing into a smooth ball and taper slightly on one side. Make an indent in the top with the frilling tool. Insert twisted green florist tape for the stalk and bend slightly; use a toothpick if required (step 5). Follow the instructions on how to glaze (page 54). Glaze the cherry.

Cover the display board

Knead the white icing to a pliable dough. Follow the instructions on how to cover a board (page 49). Stick the cake onto the board with royal icing.

It's a great idea to have a real tube of paint (or even toothpaste!) in front of you while you make this. Modelling and sculpting are always easier if you have something to copy from.

Paint tube cake

Materials
8-inch square cake
7 tablespoons syrup
3 lb 5 oz ganache
3 lb white icing (cake)
3½ oz orange icing (tube)
7 oz blue icing (tube)
1¾ oz white icing (nozzle)
3½ oz red icing (lid)
1¾ oz white icing (label)
1¾ oz red icing (letters)
2¼ lb white icing (board)
Edible silver dust
Decorating alcohol
Glaze
3½ oz red royal icing
3½ oz white royal icing
2 toothpicks
Cornstarch

Equipment
24 x 16 inch rectangular board (display)
12 x 8 inch rectangular board (set-up)
Ganaching tools (page 14)
Waxed cardboard (DIY board)
Alphabet cutters (or DIY template)
Large and small rolling pins
Pasta machine
Plastic sheets
Plastic scraper
Cranked palette knife
Flexi-scraper
Scissors
Smoother
Flexible ruler
Set of circle cutters
Frilling tool
Pizza wheel
Paintbrushes
Icing bag
No. 8 icing tip

1

2

1. Prepare the cake.

2. Shape and ganache the cake.

3. Cover the tube, nozzle and lid.

4. Make the tube colors.

5. Make the label and name stencils for the tag.

6. Pipe the oozing paint and assemble the cake.

3

4

5

6

With a set of alphabet cutters you can create any word you like. For a longer word, stick the label lengthwise down the paint tube.

Prepare the cake

The paint tube requires as much height as possible. Therefore, cut one 2-inch slice off the square and ganache it on the cake to make a 6 x 10 inch rectangle. Enlarge the template (page 188), trace on waxed paper and cut it out.

Place the template on top of the cake and with a large serrated knife, start cutting the long side of the cake to create a three-quarter round cylinder (use a real tube to copy the shape). Use the cake trim-offs to add more height where needed, sticked together with ganache.

Taper the end of the tube until it is very flat (step 2).

Cut the cylinder at the top into a dome shape (step 2). Continue cutting until the paint tube looks good from every angle.

Taper the cake at the base. Roughly ganache and allow it to set, then hot-knife the cake following the instructions on how to ganache a cake (page 38).

Make a DIY board

Trace the paint tube template on waxed cardboard and cut it out to get a DIY board (page 62). Place the cake onto the board.

Cover the cake

Knead the white icing into a pliable dough and roll out to ⅛ inch thick. Follow the instructions on how to cover a shaped cake (page 47).

Unroll the icing at the base of the tube. Keep the rounded edge at the front smooth by using two flexi-scrapers and trim the icing very neatly at the base. Use a flexible plastic ruler to push the icing in at the base. Cut the back of the tube straight. Mark indents in the icing to give it a rolled-up effect (step 3).

Make the nozzle and lid

For the nozzle, knead the white icing to a pliable dough and roll into a cylinder 2½ inches in diameter and ¾ inch thick. With the back of a knife, mark about five lines all

Pipe layers of oozing paint to create the effect of paint coming out of the tube.

around the cylinder like a nozzle thread. Keep flat until dry.

For the lid, knead the red icing to a pliable dough and roll out to ¾ inch thick. Cut a circle using a 2½-inch circle cutter. Roll out another small piece of red icing to about ⅝ inch thick and cut with a large circle cutter (about 4 inches). Stick to the top of the smaller red disc with a dab of water and mark indentations around the side with a frilling tool. Keep flat until dry.

Make the tube colors

Roll out the orange and blue icing to ⅛ inch thick. With a ruler and a pizza wheel, cut three 4½-inch wide strips, long enough to be wraped around the tube.

Brush water onto each designated area of the tube and place each strip on it, making sure to keep it straight. Brush a thin line of water in between the strips so they also join together. Smooth over with a flexi-scraper (step 4, page 174).

Make the label

Roll out the red icing in a pasta machine, or by hand, to ⅛ inch thick. Dust your work surface with a little cornstarch and place the icing on top. Let the icing dry slightly. Cut out the letters using alphabet cutters.

Roll out the white icing to ⅛ inch thick and cut it into the length and width required for letters.

Stick the letters onto the label with a dab of water (step 5, page 174).

Cover the display board

Knead the white icing to a pliable dough and roll out to ⅛ inch thick, then follow the instructions on how to cover the board (page 48), using either method.

Place the nozzle

Remember that the tube is not a complete circle, so do not place the nozzle in the center. Stick the nozzle on with royal icing. Mix the edible silver dust with decorating alcohol and paint the front and the back of the tube.

Tip: If the weather is humid the nozzle may not stick. In this case you can use toothpicks. Make a hole at the end of the nozzle with the frilling tool and stick two toothpicks through: when it is dry fasten the nozzle to the tube with the toothpicks. The toothpicks will stay in the cake so make sure to warn everyone who will eat from the cake.

Make the oozing paint

Fill an icing bag fitted with a no. 8 icing tip with the red royal icing. Pipe the "ooze," making sure to finish near the paint nozzle. Lift the icing up to the nozzle to create the effect of paint coming out of the tube. Alternatively, you can roll red icing and mold it for the same effect.

The handbag is one of the most popular cake designs at Planet Cake. You can easily personalize the monogram and colors, or incorporate the signature details of a favorite designer. Practice your quilting on a spare bit of icing before you work on the real cake.

Handbag cake

Materials
8-inch square cake
7 tablespoons syrup
3 lb 5 oz ganache
3 lb 5 oz pink icing (cake)
Wooden dowel
Two 12-inch long plastic aquarium tubing with a ½ inch diameter
Styrofoam
Toothpicks
Piping gel
1 lb 2 oz black icing (handles and decoration)
Edible gold dust
Decorating alcohol
1 lb 9 oz white icing (board)

Equipment
14-inch round board
12 x 8 inch rectangular board
Ganaching tools (page 14)
Waxed cardboard (DIY template)
Large and small rolling pins
Pasta machine
Plastic sheets
Cranked palette knife
Small kitchen knife or paring knife
Scissors
Flexi-scraper
Smoother
Plastic scraper
Pin
45° triangular ruler
Stitching tool
Medium paintbrush
Ruler
No. 4 icing tip
Pencil sharpener
Serrated dough wheel

Use your stitching tool to mark the quilting. To personalize the handbag, stick the birthday girl's initials or a favorite monogram over the quilting.

Shape and ganache the cake

Enlarge the template (page 188) on a photocopier. Trace the template for the top on waxed paper and the template for the base on waxed cardboard. Cut them out and use the waxed cardboard template as a DIY board to put underneath the cake.

Cut your square cake into three equal bricks. Ganache the three parts on top of each other, and taper the sides and build up the handbag shape with the trim-offs. Follow the instructions on how to shape a three-dimensional cake (page 41).

Once you have the required shape, ganache the whole cake. Follow the instructions on how to ganache a cake (page 38). Allow the ganache to set (step 1).

Cover the cake

Knead the pink icing to a pliable dough and roll out to ⅛ inch thick. Cover the cake, pinching at the sides and trimming away the excess with a small sharp knife and scissors. Smooth the cake and trim the icing at the base and edges (step 2).

Mark the quilting

While the icing is still soft and starting from the left side crease, use a pin to mark the icing every 1½ inches along the base (the last section may not be the exact size, but that is all right). Repeat on the other side (the back) of the cake.

Using the triangular ruler and starting from the left side, place the short side onto the board at the first pin mark and glide the back of your paring knife along the edge of the triangle to mark a line to the top of the cake. Repeat at each pin mark.

Once all the lines are marked, repeat the same method starting at the right side (step 3) to create the quilting effect. Run the stitching tool along the lines to create the stitching marks (step 3).

Make the handles

Cut four lengths of wooden dowels thick enough to fit snugly into the ends of the plastic tubing (if too thin use toothpicks as fillers) to 4 inches long. Push 1 inch of the dowel into both ends of the tubes. Sharpen the other ends of the dowel with a

pencil sharpener and poke them into a piece of styrofoam 6 inches apart (step 4). Brush the tubes with piping gel.

Roll out 10½ oz of the black icing to about ⅛ inch thick and cut a strip 12 inches long and 1½ inches wide. Cover the strips with plastic to prevent from drying out. Stick the strips around the tubes with piping gel, using your fingers to smooth the icing. Trim away any excess with scissors or a knife and smooth with your fingers or a flexi-scraper. Leave to dry.

Note: Since your are using plastic tubes as a base for the handles, the handles won't be edible. Therefore, make sure not to serve them.

Make the zipper

Roll out ¾ oz of the left-over pink icing to ⅛ inch thick. Cut two strips as long as the top of the handbag, one 1 inch wide and the other ¼ inch wide. Cover the wider strip with plastic. Run a serrated dough wheel along the thin strip to mark a zipper line (page 60).

1. Shape and ganache the cake.

2. Cover the cake.

3. Mark the quilted pattern on the sides of the handbag.

4. Make the handles.

5. Make the zipper, the decorative triangle and the monogram.

6. Assemble the cake.

Paint the zipper with gold dust mixed with decorating alcohol to create a metallic look.

Use a ruler and stitching tool to mark a line on both edges of the wider strip. Stick the thinner strip on top of the wider strip and stick the zipper on the handbag with a little water. Trim any excess.

Roll a small pink icing ball to the size of a pea and mold it into a rectangle lightly tapered to one side. Stick it on top of the zipper.

Make the tongue of the zipper the same way, without tapering the rectangle. Cut out a hole with the no. 4 icing tip and let it dry. Stick it on the tapered rectangle (step 5, page 181). Mix the edible gold dust with decorating alcohol and brush it over the zipper using a paintbrush.

Place the handles

To make sure the handles are positioned in the center of the handbag, measure the zipper to find its center and then measure 3 inches to either side of the center. Mark the icing with a pin. Stick the wooden dowels into the holes.

Remember that the cake is tapered. If you poke the dowel straight down you might pierce the side of the cake and make a hole. Repeat with the other handle. Make four rolls of black icing about ½ inch thick and about 8 inches long. Knot them around the base of the handles.

Make the monogram and triangle

For the triangle, roll out 1¾ oz of the black icing to about ⅛ inch thick. Using the template (page 188), cut out the side-trim triangle. Brush some water on the cake and stick the triangle on, trim the edges and smooth either with your finger or the flexi-scraper (step 5, page 181).

For the monogram, use the template in this book (page 188) or any you like and enlarge it to the size you want. Roll out black icing to about ⅛ inch thick. Cut the letters from the icing with a small knife and stick them on the cake with a dab of water (step 5).

Cover the display board

Enlarge the template for the base (page 188) on a photocopier, trace on waxed paper and cut it out. Follow the instructions on how to cover the board around the cake (page 51).

Roll out the white icing to ⅛ inch thick and about 2 inches larger than the size of the board. Put the template on the icing and cut around it, then take the center piece out.

Cut a slit in the remaining icing to allow access for the cake. As if you were fitting a horseshoe, place the icing onto the board around the cake making sure the slit is at the back. Ensure the icing meets perfectly at the back, overlap the icing and re-cut the slit (page 51).

Dampen the board with water or syrup to make the icing stick to the board, then smooth the icing with the flexi-scraper. Use an acrylic smoother or flexi-scraper to trim the icing at the end of the board.

Templates

All the templates you need for the cakes
appear in this section. Each template is marked
with the percentage of enlargement required to
create the correct size on a photocopier.

Make-up box cake
Indentation stencil for
the make-up box
page 132
Enlarge by 166%

Princess cake
page 104
Enlarge by 166%

Boot cake
page 154
Enlarge by 200%

Airplane cake
page 160
Enlarge by 200%

handle

tie

tie

tie

Briefcase cake
page 118
Enlarge by 200%

Giant cupcake
page 168

Icing top
Enlarge by 333%

Flip flop cake
page 146
Enlarge by 250%

Pirate cake
page 96
Enlarge by 300%

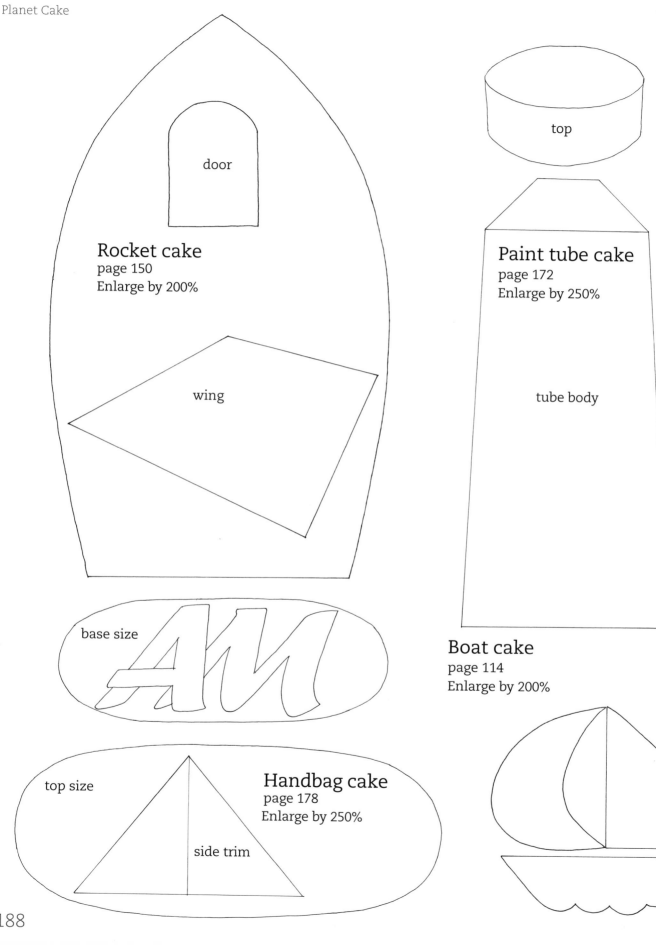

Rocket cake
page 150
Enlarge by 200%

door

wing

Paint tube cake
page 172
Enlarge by 250%

top

tube body

Boat cake
page 114
Enlarge by 200%

base size

Handbag cake
page 178
Enlarge by 250%

top size

side trim

Ice-cream cake
page 142

Melting chocolate
Enlarge by 250%

Record player cake
page 126

Indentation for the record player

Actual size

bite

Ice-cream cake
page 142
Enlarge by 250%

ice-cream stick

Racing car cake
page 92
Enlarge by 200%

wheel

wheel

Index

METRO BOOKS
New York

An Imprint of Sterling Publishing
387 Park Avenue South
New York, NY 10016

© 2009 by Murdoch Books Pty Limited

This 2009 edition published by Metro Books,
by arrangement with Murdoch Books Pty Limited.

Editors: Kristin Buesing, Glenda Downing
Sandra Loy (US edition)
Designer: Marylouise Brammer
Photographer: Natasha Milne
Stylist: Kate Brown
Illustrator: Margaret Carter
Production: Alexandra Gonzalez

ISBN 978-1-4351-1705-1

For information about custom editions, special sales, and premium and corporate purchases, please contact Sterling Special Sales at 800-805-5489 or specialsales@sterlingpublishing.com.

Manufactured in China.

4 6 8 10 9 7 5 3

www.sterlingpublishing.com

IMPORTANT: Those who might be at risk from the effects of salmonella poisoning (the elderly, pregnant women, young children and those suffering from immune deficiency diseases) should consult their doctor with any concerns about eating raw eggs.

OVEN GUIDE: You may find cooking times vary depending on the oven you are using. For fan-forced ovens, as a general rule, set the oven temperature to 35°F lower than indicated in the recipe.